LEISUREGUIDE

Hampshire

including
The New Forest

AA Publishing

Contents

Author: Helen Livingston

Walks: David Hancock

Designer: Stuart Perry

Produced by AA Publishing
© Automobile Association
Developments Ltd 1996, 2002.

Published by AA Publishing (a trading name of Automobile Association Developments Limited, whose registered office is Millstream, Maidenhead Road, Windsor, Berkshire, SL4 5GD. Registered Number 1878835)

First edition published 1996, reprinted 1996, 1997.
Second edition 2002.

Mapping produced by the Cartographic Department of The Automobile Association. A00691.

ISBN 07495 3294 7

A CIP catalogue record for this book is available from the British Library.

Gazetteer map references are taken from the National Grid and can be used in conjunction with Ordnance Survey maps and atlases. Places featured in this guide will not necessarily be found on the maps at the back of the book.

All the walks are on rights of way, permissive paths or on routes where de facto access for walkers is accepted. On routes which are not on legal rights of way, but where access for walkers is allowed by local agreements, no implication of a right of way is intended.

The contents of this book are believed correct at the time of printing. Nevertheless, the publishers cannot accept responsibility for errors or omissions, or for changes in details given in this guide or for the consequences of any reliance on the information it provides. We have tried to ensure accuracy in this book, but things do change and we would be grateful if readers would advise us of any inaccuracies they may encounter.

Visit the AA Publishing website at www.theAA.com

Colour reproduction by L C Repro

Printed and bound by G. Canale & C. s.p.a., Torino, Italy

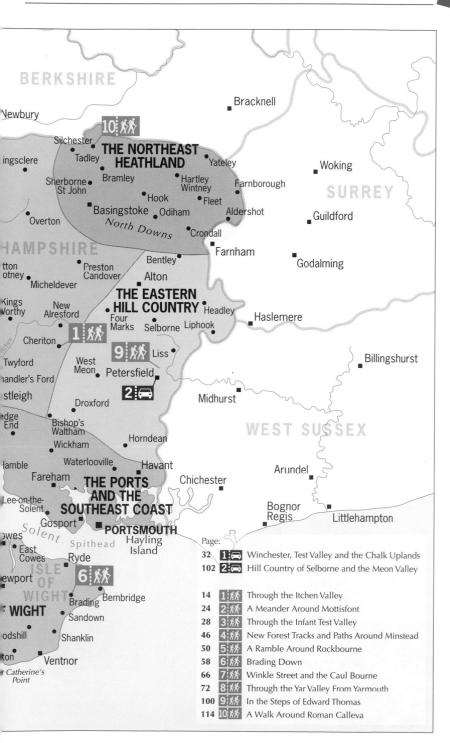

BERKSHIRE

Newbury

Bracknell

Silchester

10 **THE NORTHEAST HEATHLAND**

Tadley

ingsclere

Yateley

Woking

SURREY

Sherborne
St John

Bramley

Hartley
Wintney

Farnborough

Hook

Fleet

Aldershot

Guildford

Basingstoke

Odiham

Overton

North Downs

Crondall

HAMPSHIRE

Bentley

Farnham

Godalming

tton
otney

Preston
Candover

Alton

Micheldever

Kings
Worthy

New
Alresford

THE EASTERN HILL COUNTRY

Headley

Haslemere

Four
Marks

Selborne

Liphook

1 Cheriton

9 Liss

Billingshurst

Twyford

West
Meon

Petersfield

handler's Ford

stleigh

2

Droxford

Midhurst

dge
End

Bishop's
Waltham

WEST SUSSEX

Horndean

Wickham

Hamble

Waterlooville

Havant

Chichester

Arundel

Fareham

Lee-on-the-
Solent

THE PORTS AND THE SOUTHEAST COAST

Gosport

PORTSMOUTH

Bognor
Regis

Littlehampton

Solent

owes

East
Cowes

Spithead

Hayling
Island

Ryde

ISLE
OF
WIGHT

6

ewport

Brading

Bembridge

WIGHT

Sandown

odshill

Shanklin

ton

Ventnor

Catherine's
Point

Introducing Hampshire and The New Forest

THE VICTORY
Hampshire's coastal ports are steeped in history, and from tiny harbours to naval cities they offer an insight in to the seafaring traditions of England

The lure of Hampshire is not easy to define, for it is a county of contrasts and has many aspects: ancient and modern, rural and urban – and in this infinite variety lies its unfailing magic. Winchester, Alfred the Great's historic capital, lies very much at the centre, while to north and west stretch vast chalk uplands, threaded by numerous streams renowned for trout; to the southwest are the New Forest woodlands and heaths; on the east are steep chalk hills with hanging beech woods; sandy heaths rich with pines and birch crowd into the northeast; the south coast throbs with the busy ports of Southampton and Portsmouth, which both have fascinating stories to tell, while across the Solent, beloved of sailors, is the pleasant Isle of Wight. There are great houses; historic ecclesiastical buildings, pleasant country towns; little villages tucked in hidden places and big bold viewpoints.

THE NEW FOREST
A pleasing mixture of ancient woodland and open heath, with the famous semi-wild ponies always near

GILBERT WHITE
His Natural History of Selborne, published in 1789 did much to popularise the study of wildlife

A FAWN IN THE FOREST
Wild deer are to be found in woodland throughout Hampshire, although they are shy creatures and you will be lucky to see them

MAN AND MONUMENT
Alfred, Lord Tennyson made his home on the Isle of Wight, and a memorial to him stands on the downland which he loved

READY FOR DUTY
Carisbrooke Castle was once famous for the labour of its prisoners; now a donkey turns the c1580 well winding wheel instead

FLYING THE ARMY WAY
The Museum of Army Flying at Middle Wallop offers a microcosm of flight history, with early rotorcraft as well as fixed wing aircraft

TOP TEN ATTRACTIONS

Winchester Cathedral
Mottisfont Gardens and the Test Valley
Lymington Market
The Isle of Wight
Milestones
Old Portsmouth and the Historic Ships
Selborne and The Hanger
The View from Old Winchester Hill
Roman Silchester
Alresford and The Watercress Line

A CREST FROM THE PAST
Winchester is steeped in history and well worth exploring, from the cathedral to its famous public school

THE ESSENCE OF HAMPSHIRE AND THE NEW FOREST

If you have little time and want to sample the essence of Hampshire:

Explore historic Winchester Cathedral and Romsey Abbey... **Drive** down the Test valley from Stockbridge to Mottisfont Abbey and Gardens ... **Climb** Old Winchester Hill, with its panoramic views ... **Visit** Old Portsmouth with its historic ships ... **Indulge** yourself with dinner at Gordleton Mill in Lymington ... **Visit** Selborne, home of Gilbert White, and follow his footsteps up Selborne Hill ... **Have a picnic** in the New Forest then take a horse-drawn wagon ride along one of the ornamental drives ... **Go shopping** in Lymington's 700-year-old street market ... If you have time **take the ferry** over the Solent from Lymington to Yarmouth on the Isle of Wight ... **Treat yourself** to a drink at the remote White Horse, near Petersfield, utterly rural and old fashioned.

GOLDEN VIEWS
In early summer the heath and downland of Hampshire is gilded with the brilliant flowers of broom, left

DELIGHTS OF THE DOWNS
The chalk downs of Hampshire support many varieties of butterfly including the Chalkhill Blue

JANE AUSTEN
Born at Steventon near Basingstoke in 1775 and buried in Winchester. Her house at Chawton is now a modest museum

HAMPSHIRE HOPS
An Alton inn sign reminds that Hampshire has a famous presence in the brewing industry

TOP TROUT
The clear waters of the Test, the Itchen and the Hampshire Avon provide some of the best fishing in Britain

A Weekend in Hampshire and the New Forest

For many of us a weekend is the most that can be managed as a break in busy lives. These four pages offer an itinerary designed to ensure that you see and enjoy the very best of both the historic and maritime Hampshire, including a trip over to the Isle of Wight. Places with gazetteer entries are in **bold**.

Friday Night

If you can afford it, stay at the world-famous Chewton Glen Hotel at New Milton, for sheer luxury and excellent food in grand country house surroundings. The Chewton Glen ranks among the very best hotels in the country, but if it is too formal, or too expensive, Lymington has lots of very good alternatives.

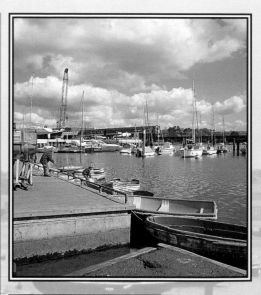

Saturday Morning

Start the day with a breezy 30-minute ferry trip from **Lymington** to **Yarmouth** – the best crossing to the Isle of Wight. This is just a brief visit so, unless you prefer to spend the whole day here, leave your car in Lymington. Browse around this small historic port and sample the special atmosphere of the island before returning to Lymington, then go for a stroll up the High Street, with its famous 700-year-old market.

Lymington is a great centre for exploring the New Forest or for hopping across to the Isle of Wight

Take time to view Beaulieu Abbey, above, and don't miss Buckler's Hard, right

Saturday Lunch

Take the B3054 over Beaulieu Heath to **Beaulieu** for lunch at the Montagu Arms, a lovely old creeper-clad hotel with terraced gardens and fine food.

Saturday Afternoon

Spend the afternoon exploring the National Motor Museum, Palace House and Abbey ruins at Lord Montagu's ancestral home, and if there is time head down to **Buckler's Hard**, the historic shipbuilding centre with a maritime museum.

Complete the day with a drive through the New Forest, along the B3056 to **Lyndhurst,** the capital of the New Forest, then north along the A337. When you reach the A31, turn east, avoiding the M27, and follow the road through **Romsey** (with its historic abbey) and continue to **Winchester.**

Saturday Night

Stay at Lainston House, a fine country hotel to the west of the city near Sparsholt, or if you wish to stay in the city, go for the Hotel du Vin, an elegant townhouse, which is quietly situated, but central to all Winchester's many attractions. Both hotels offer very good food.

Above and right, combine a visit to the New Forest with a glimpse of Romsey Abbey, and go on to Winchester, far right

Day Two: Winchester and the River Test

This is the day for exploring one of Britain's most historic and interesting cities before heading out into the wonderful Test Valley. If it rains, stay in Winchester, where there are more than enough under-cover attractions to fill the day.

Sunday Morning

After breakfast, take a leisurely walk around Winchester, the former capital of England and one of the most historic towns in Britain. There is a lot to see, including the cathedral, High Street, the Westgate and many museums.

In the late morning, head westwards, following the old Roman road up on to the hills past **Farley Mount** and the country park, then on to Kings Somborne and the neighbouring village of Horsebridge.

Stroll around Winchester at your leisure, left, then head out into the countryside of the Test Valley, below

Sunday Lunch

Stop for lunch at the John of Gaunt pub in Horsebridge, which has well prepared fresh food. Here you are right on the **River Test**, perhaps the most famous trout fishing river in the world – beloved of Izaak Walton, it is certainly one of the most beautiful rivers in Britain.

Sunday Afternoon

If the weather is kind, take a gentle afternoon stroll up the Test Way and then along the Clarendon Way over the Test into Houghton. These stretches are fished by the exclusive Houghton Club, one of the oldest fishing clubs in Britain – it only ever has 17 members.

Above, follow the river to Mottisfont with its abbey and gardens, right, and continue to Stockbridge, below

If you have time, visit **Mottisfont**, with its abbey and gardens, further down the Test Valley, then head north again to **Stockbridge,** surrounded by hills and with its delightful wide main street crossed by branches of the Test. Lots of scope for an excellent afternoon tea here, and plenty of antique shops and galleries to browse around before heading for home.

Winchester and the Chalk Uplands

Winchester, England's ancient capital, lies amid rolling chalkland scenery, with roads radiating outwards from it across the county. It is very much the centre of Hampshire, both physically and spiritually. Around it, particularly to the north and west, are two contrasting landscapes: the wide serene chalklands of 'High Hampshire', lonely and open, dotted here and there with clumps of dark green yews and graceful beeches, and the fisherman's Hampshire — shallow green valleys of water meadows and sparkling streams that bring anglers from the four winds to try their skill in England's most famous trout rivers. This is an area of unhurried little roads, great houses and gardens, tranquil rivers and sweeping views.

HAMPSHIRE WATERCRESS

Watercress needs to be planted submerged in gently flowing shallow water if it is to be grown to perfection, and few places are possessed with exactly the right conditions. The Hampshire chalklands with their sparkling streams fit the bill precisely, particularly around Alresford where the plants flourish in specially constructed beds alongside the streams. Watercress needs to be consumed soon after it is picked because it wilts easily; the Watercress Line, now a preserved steam railway, originally carried the harvest to London markets; today container lorries transport it to the European market.

Alresford's leafy Broad Street leads down the hill to an ancient bridge

ALRESFORD   Map ref SU5832

Lovely Alresford, with its wide streets of friendly Georgian houses of brick and stucco, lies in the broad valley of the River Alre, hence the name (pronounced 'Allsford'). It is really two places – Old Alresford to the north of the river, which is no more than a village with an adjoining park, and New Alresford, the busy market town to the south which was 'New' in about 1200. Between the two is Alresford Pond, created by Bishop de Lucy in the 13th century. Its dam, the Great Weir, is the largest non-military medieval earthwork in England and the only one that still serves this original dual purpose of dam and road causeway.

Today its 30 acres are a haven for wildlife and also feed the famous local watercress beds.

New Alresford retains its medieval street plan, with a T-shape formed by the spacious elegant Broad Street and West and East Streets, the old Winchester–London road. Becoming a borough in 1294, New Alresford soon became one of England's ten greatest wool markets. Two of its mills survive, the Town Mill and the old Fulling Mill. A series of fires devastated New Alresford between the early 15th century and 1689, which accounts for its mainly Georgian appearance.

Approach from Old Alresford or from Bishop's Sutton to get the best introduction to the town – the south approach from Cheriton leads through less inviting modern suburbs. Strolling through New Alresford is a delight. The town has a variety of interesting shops and some excellent craft workshops, and Broad Street, with its lime trees and old fashioned lamps, is undoubtedly one of Hampshire's best streets.

Mary Russell Mitford, author of the classic *Our Village* was born at 27 Broad Street in 1787 and lived there until she was ten, when she moved with her father to Three Mile Cross near Reading – the village of her book. She later wrote 'Alresford is or will be celebrated in history for two things: the first, to speak modestly, is my birth, the second is cricket'. Few today would associate Alresford with cricket, but Taylor of Alresford, a member of the famous Hambledon Club was born here, and cricket writer and commentator John Arlott once lived at the Old Sun. Today Alresford is better known for its watercress beds and its steam railway, the Watercress Line.

THE WATERCRESS LINE

The Mid-Hants Railway received its nickname in the days when freshly picked watercress was carried by train to be sold. There are gradients up to 1-in-60 on the line, giving rise to the local saying that the line runs 'over the Alps'! The line opened in 1865, carrying trains through from Southampton to Guildford, but the watercress trade switched to road transport in 1963 and the line closed ten years later. Today ten miles (16km) of the line between Alresford and Alton (where it connects with the main line) is run as a preserved steam railway, with intermediate stations at Medstead & Four Marks and Ropley. Steam locomotives in various stages of restoration can be seen at the stations.

During World War I the Watercress Line linked Aldershot directly with Southampton Docks

Through the Itchen Valley

This route follows the Wayfarer's Walk/Itchen Way close to the banks of the delightful Itchen before venturing up on to downland with scenic views. The walk features two charming settlements, notably the mainly thatched and peaceful village of Tichborne. Muddy farm and woodland tracks, otherwise good well waymarked paths.

Time: 3 hours. Distance: 6½ miles (10.5km).
Location: 2 miles (3.2km) south of New Alresford.
Start: Park in Cheriton village centre, off the B3046.
(OS grid ref: SU583285.)
OS Map: Explorer 132 (Winchester, New Alresford & East Meon) 1:25,000.
See Key to Walks on page 121.

ROUTE DIRECTIONS

From **Cheriton** post office on the lane off the B3046, walk north passing a side lane to the school, then take the **Wayfarer's Walk** arrowed left beside cottages and cross the B-road on to a metalled no through road, signed 'Hill Houses Lane'. Shortly, go through the waymarked stile on the right and keep to the right-hand field edge to a further stile. Keep right through two more pastures via stiles, parallel to the River Itchen, to a stile and pass beside Cheriton Mill to a lane.

Turn right, then left at the T-junction with B3046 and shortly turn left through a gap in the hedge (The Itchen Way). Bear half-right, with Tichborne church visible on the horizon, to a stile. Proceed across the next field to a stile flanking a gate into a strip of woodland.

Climb a further stile, keep left through parkland to a stile by the gates to Tichborne House and proceed over the crossroads. In 100 yards (91 metres) where the drive veers sharp left, keep ahead beside woodland, then in 400 yards (366 metres) bear off right through some trees and maintain direction along a path between fields. Cross two stiles and turn left, parallel with the main road (A31).

Remain on this defined path which bears left, eventually passing Vernal Farm and crossing the river to a road. Cross over and follow the path uphill along the left-hand field edge. At the top corner, go through a gap in the hedge and turn left downhill keeping to the defined track to enter the village of **Tichborne**.

Just before the lane, take the narrow path right, uphill to **St Andrew's Church**. Bear left past the Old School House, then turn right on to a high-hedged track and keep left along the edge of a large field, eventually bearing left to a stile in the hedge. Bear half-right to a stile near a barn and turn right up a stony track, passing two further barns to a gate.

Go through the gate, fork left and follow the field edge, then ascend to a gate and enter a wood. Keep to the meandering main path, exit via a gap and bear left along a metalled farm road. At a junction of tracks, keep straight on into the hamlet of Hill Houses and follow the lane downhill back into Cheriton.

A picturesque cowl of thatch smothers cottages in Tichborne

POINTS OF INTEREST

Cheriton

Despite the presence of the B-road this attractive village retains a peaceful charm, with several picturesque thatched cottages, a green with a duck pond and the River Itchen. Its ancient church stands on what is thought to be a prehistoric burial ground. The village is known for the Battle of Cheriton in 1644, near Cheriton Wood (1 mile/ 1.6km west), where 2,000 men were killed as the Roundheads defeated the Royalists.

Wayfarer's Walk

This long-distance footpath, with a WW logo, traverses the heart of Hampshire, linking Inkpen Beacon in the north to Emsworth on the coast in the south.

Tichborne

An unspoilt picture-postcard village of mainly half-timbered thatched cottages famous for the story of the 'Tichborne Dole'. This tradition dates from the time of Henry I, when the owner of Tichborne Park, Sir Roger Tichborne, made a callous promise to his bedridden wife that she could provide funds for the needy, but only within an area that she could crawl around. He obviously underestimated her determination for she managed to encircle about 20 acres – known to this day as The Crawls. Since then local residents have received a bag of flour from the owners of Tichborne Park every year in March.

St Andrew's Church

This 900-year-old building is unique in Hampshire in having a Roman Catholic chapel within an Anglican church. The chancel is Norman, and the fine high box-pews are Jacobean.

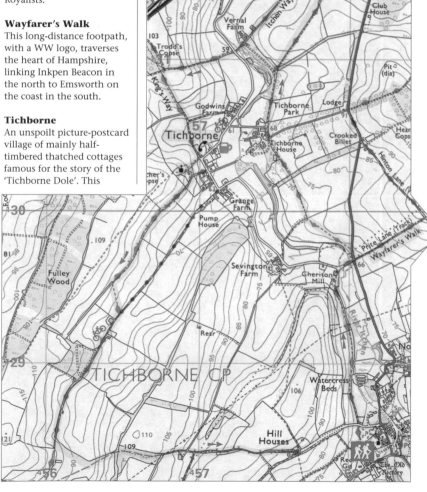

Hillier Arboretum offers foliage for all seasons

'HAMPSHIRE WEED'

Dark, impenetrable evergreen yew, a conifer native to chalk downlands, grows large and lush around Winchester and northwestern Hampshire, so much so that it has become known as 'Hampshire weed', in rather the same way that the clay-loving oak tree is known as the 'Sussex weed' or beeches are native to the Buckinghamshire Chilterns. Famous Hampshire yews include the avenue leading to a vanished house near Preston Candover, which was much admired by William Cobbett. Since yews are poisonous they have to be grown out of the reach of cattle.

AMPFIELD Map ref SU4023

In wooded country west of Winchester, this little village, set among beech woods and cornfields, is famed for the nearby Hillier Gardens and Arboretum. Sir Harold Hillier, the great plantsman, began his famous and unique collection of trees and shrubs in 1953, a collection which was to become one of the largest of its kind in the world, with some 40,000 temperate plants originating from every continent. There is colour at every season of the year with witch hazels, rhododendrons, herbaceous perennials and autumn foliage.

The heart of the village is at Knapp, now designated a conservation area. There were clay pits and a pottery near by, and the Potters Heron Hotel preserves in its name a shadowy recollection of the old industry, since a potter's treadle wheel is also known as a 'hern' or 'heron'. In much later times this same clay was used to make the bricks for the Church of St Mark, built 1838–41 at the instigation of John Keble, a famous member of the High Church Oxford Movement, who was vicar at nearby Hursley.

Ampfield has literary associations. Richard Morley, the 17th-century 'Hedge Poet', lived here and The Rev W Awdry, author of Thomas the Tank Engine books, spent his boyhood in Ampfield, where his father was the vicar.

AVINGTON PARK Map ref SU5432

Avington Park, probably dating from the early 18th century, is a big rose-pink house with a splendid portico and some wonderful interior features, including a painted ceiling by Verrio and a fine colonnade in the 19th-century conservatory. In November 1825 William Cobbett rode through on the little road from Easton, passing the spot where today there is a pleasant picnic site. He described the scene in *Rural Rides* and the description still fits, though perhaps Cobbett exaggerated the abundance of the water fowl! '... The house is close down at the edge of the meadow land; there is a lawn before it, and a pond supplied by the Itchen, ... and we saw thousands of wild ducks in the pond or sitting round on the green edges of it ... We looked down on all this from a rising ground, and the water, like a looking-glass, showed us the trees, and even the animals. This certainly is one of the prettiest spots in the world ...' The views to the house across the lake and parkland are little changed since those days.

The brick-built Church of St Mary was built in 1768–71 by Margaret, Marchioness of Carnarvon. It preserves the air of the 18th century as verily as the view over the park. A large monument to the Marchioness (died 1768) is in pink and white marble with two urns and an obelisk, and another monument is to John Shelley (died 1866), brother of the famous poet.

ROYAL ASSIGNATIONS
Avington Park's owner, George Brydges, had as his patron no less a personage than Charles II. The king and his mistress, Nell Gwynn, would stay at Avington during the six weeks of Winchester's racing season. More royal assignations were reputed to have taken place here about 150 years later, when George IV would meet up with his mistress, Mrs Fitzherbert.

The River Itchen broadens attractively into a lake at Avington Park

THE SILVER ROUTE OF THE ROMAN EMPIRE

The Roman road from the Mendip mines via Old Sarum and Winchester crosses Farley Mount. This road was used to transport the silver-bearing lead to Bitterne, now a suburb of Southampton, for shipment to the Roman Imperial Mint at Lyon. Today, this important road can be traced eastwards as an embankment under the trees, but nearer Winchester it is followed by the present-day Sarum Road.

The modern road crosses the river in about the same place as the old Roman road. This crossing point remained the most important for centuries after the Romans left, and was used by many English kings, notably King John, when they rode to Winchester to the Palace of Clarendon and to great hunting forests.

The extraordinary frescoes of the Sandham Memorial Chapel reflect the artist's own experiences as a Red Cross orderly during World War I

BURGHCLERE   Map ref SU4761

Burghclere lies in the wooded vale below the chalk uplands of northern Hampshire, a rather dispersed place, with old cottages sprinkled here and there among the many newer houses. Its claim to fame is the Sandham Memorial Chapel (National Trust) with murals by Stanley Spencer, commissioned by Mr and Mrs J L Behrend to commemorate Lieutenant H W Sandham. He died in 1919 of an illness contracted on the Macedonian Campaign in World War I.

The artist had been an orderly on the campaign, and the paintings are based on his sketches at the time. Executed in 1927–32 in Spencer's own expressionist style, they make a dramatic impact. The scenes depicted consist mostly of ordinary soldiers going about the mundane and everyday tasks of war, but the east wall is covered by a magnificent mural of the resurrection of the dead soldiers, showing them rising from their graves, shaking hands, and bearing their crosses towards a diminutive figure of the risen Christ, who stands above to receive them.

FARLEY MOUNT   Map ref SU4029

Farley Mount Country Park covers over 1,000 acres of chalk upland west of Winchester and east of the broad Test valley. At 586 feet, it is the highest point in the region and possesses wonderful views in all directions. The country park is known for its variety of habitats, with short turf, ancient woodland and Forestry Commission plantation. There is plenty of wildlife in the oak, beech and yew woods and in the sea of ancient coppicing. Orchids are plentiful and there are a number of nature trails in Crab Wood, on the east side of the park. There are several car parks and a picnic site. The park is crossed by the Roman road from the Mendip silver-lead mines and Old Sarum to Winchester.

HIGHCLERE CASTLE Map ref SU4549

This splendid Victorian house, the largest mansion in Hampshire, is the home of the Earl and Countess of Carnarvon. The house was rebuilt for the then earl in the 1840s by Sir Charles Barry, architect of the Houses of Parliament – a grandiose Elizabethan-style three-storeyed mansion with angle-turrets and a big, pinnacled tower in the centre. It stands proudly in the old park, landscaped by Lancelot 'Capability' Brown.

The internal decoration is extraordinarily rich and varied with Gothic, Moorish and rococo styles rubbing shoulders and yet blending together, all permeated with the ornate atmosphere of High Victorianism. The library is probably the best room in the house, 18th century in character, with a screen of fluted Ionic columns that separate it from the North Library. The wealth of artefacts displayed in the house includes a collection of old masters and an exhibition of Egyptian antiquities collected by the 5th Earl who, with Howard Carter, discovered the tomb of Tutankhamun.

The life of servants in Victorian times is depicted in the appropriate rooms, and there is a racing exhibition, put together by the present earl, Her Majesty the Queen's Racing Manager. Highclere Castle has been the location of several film and television productions including *The Secret Garden, Inspector Morse, Jeeves and Wooster, The Secret Life of Ian Fleming* and *The Free Frenchmen.*

The splendid mansion of Highclere Castle hosts spectacular summer events

THE HIDDEN HOARD

After the death of the 6th Earl of Carnarvon a remarkable discovery was made by the family butler – a hidden chamber between the drawing room and the smoking room. Its doors had been locked and blocked by heavy furniture some 67 years earlier and when they were opened revealed a collection of ancient artefacts brought back by the 5th Earl from his expeditions to Egypt. Even his son had not known of their existence. The finds are now on display in the basement of Highclere Castle.

IRON-AGE SITES

The area around Andover is particularly rich in Iron-Age sites – one of the greatest concentrations in Europe. Danebury was a hillfort of the British tribe of Atrebates, and was occupied around 550–100 BC. It housed over 200 people and their animals, and there is evidence of considerable agricultural activity as well as pottery and metalworking. Shale and salt found here suggest that trade was developing and that Danebury was very close to being a true town. Andover's Museum of the Iron Age reconstructs Iron-Age life with tools, implements, weapons, querns and a replica loom, laying particular emphasis on Danebury, with a replica of the outer defences and an Iron-Age round house.

Displays at the Museum of Army Flying include aircraft of all types

HINTON AMPNER Map ref SU6027

The name comes from 'hea-tun', the village on high ground, with 'Ampner' a corruption of 'Almoner', since during the Middle Ages the manor belonged to the Almoner of St Swithun's Priory, Winchester.

At the Reformation it passed to the Stawell family. The manor house, church, rectory and a few farmhouses and cottages make a classic English group in beautiful rolling countryside, yet Hinton Ampner has seen weird goings on. The Tudor house that stood near the site of the present one was so severely haunted as to be uninhabitable, since anyone who tried to live there was driven out by the ghosts. The only solution was to demolish the house, and this was carried out in 1793. During the demolition a baby's skull was found in a box under the floorboards, giving credence to the local belief that the ghosts were those of Lord Stawell and his sister-in-law, and the skull that of their illegitimate child whom they had murdered.

The Georgian manor house (National Trust) built in its place was gutted by fire in 1960, but has been rebuilt. Fine Regency furniture, pictures and porcelain are on display, while the gardens are a pleasant mixture of formal and informal, with delightful walks and unexpected views.

MIDDLE WALLOP Map ref SU2937

The Museum of Army Flying is just along the main road from Middle Wallop beside the Army Air Corps Airfield and houses a unique collection of aircraft, World War II gliders and helicopters, with dioramas and exhibitions. The story begins with pre-World War I balloons and kites, continues with World War I aviators and then the story of the airfield as a World War II Battle of Britain fighter station. Middle Wallop houses the archives of the Glider Pilot Regiment and the many gliders on show include 'Horsa', 'Wacco' and the enormous tank-carrier, 'Hamilcar'. The museum includes a number of simulated 'hands on' displays.

Middle Wallop is the middle of three villages in the valley of the Wallop Brook, a tributary of the River Test, and a delightful, stream-filled valley it is. Nether Wallop, set among the alders and water meadows, is the most beautiful of the villages, and its church contains 11th-century wall paintings showing not only Christ in Majesty, but also – unusually – St George fighting the dragon. On the chalk hill to the east is the Iron-Age site of Danebury Hillfort.

MOTTISFONT ABBEY   Map ref SU3226

The little village of Mottisfont lies in that part of the wide green Test valley where the trees seem to be exceptionally large, the streams of the river particularly numerous and the atmosphere breathes peace and prosperity. The name is derived from the spring or 'font' which rises where the village 'moot' was held in Saxon times. (See Walk on page 24.)

A house of Augustinian canons was founded here in 1201, which at the Dissolution passed to Lord Sandys, in exchange for the then villages of Paddington and Chelsea! Unusually, it was the church that he converted into his mansion, demolishing the residential parts of the priory. The Tudor building was remodelled in the 18th century by the Mills family, to whom it had passed, giving rise to the beautiful mellow house of today. It was given to the National Trust in 1957 and is famed for its drawing room, decorated by Rex Whistler and Derek Hill's 20th-century picture collection. The beautiful tranquil grounds have sweeping lawns which run down to the River Test and the walled garden houses the National Collection of old roses.

OPEN-AIR THEATRE
Plays are staged in the grounds of Mottisfont Abbey during June and July, and there are occasionally concerts too. The location on the lawns is particularly enchanting and the plays move from lawn to lawn. The theatre used to be run by an outside group, but is now under the aegis of the National Trust. The programme of events is issued sometime in the spring.

Mottisfont Abbey has beautiful gardens, including a superb collection of old-fashioned roses

*The dramatic shell of
Northington Grange*

THE WAYFARER'S WALK
This exhilarating 70-mile
(112.7-km) path runs from
Emsworth to Inkpen Beacon,
just inside Berkshire. Passing
through Havant, it swings
round Portsmouth and heads
up the Meon Valley before
climbing on to the chalklands
to pass the source of the River
Itchen. Beyond the Candover
Valley it climbs into High
Hampshire, with wonderful
views across the Kennet Vale,
crossing Watership Down
along the way. Made famous
in Richard Adams' modern
classic about a rabbit colony,
the down is now a nature
reserve, with plenty of rabbits.

NORTHINGTON GRANGE   Map ref SU5636
The Grange (English Heritage) has been described as 'the
most important neo-Classical country house in Europe',
and yet it is miraculous that it has survived at all. It was
built in 1809–16 by the 24-year-old William Wilkins, just
back from a tour of Greece and Asia Minor and fired by
all he had seen. He encased the existing 17th-century
house in a Grecian-style shell, and then fronted the
eastern elevation with a huge portico of Doric columns,
based on the Temple of Theseus in Athens.

The Grange's heyday was after 1817 when it was
bought by Lord Ashburton, and it was still a residence in
the 1930s, but by 1970 it had been gutted and was in
danger of collapse. It was rescued by the government in
1975 and, though it remains an empty shell, the exterior
has been restored to its former glory. Magnificent opera
events are now staged here in June.

RIVER ITCHEN
The River Itchen, famed for watercress beds and trout
fishing, rises in a little hollow just west of Hinton
Ampner and flows for 25 miles to the sea at
Southampton. Past Tichborne (see Walk on page 14), it
gathers the waters of its main tributary, the River Alre,
just west of Alresford. Here the river begins its habit of

dividing into a number of streamlets and enters its best trout fishing reaches at Ovington and Avington, where there are good walks in the peaceful water meadows. The river breaks through the chalk hills at Winchester to continue past Eastleigh and the Itchen Valley Country Park to Southampton. The Itchen Navigation, a canal in use between 1710 and 1869, runs for ten miles from Wharf Hill, Winchester to Southampton. There are good walks alongside it, and The Itchen Way follows the river from source to mouth.

RIVER TEST

The 'Queen of the Chalk Streams' is world famous for its trout fishing – there are waiting lists for the two famous, and expensive, clubs, which control fishing on the river above and below Stockbridge. In its lower reaches the Test is also a salmon river, and there are angling facilities at Romsey. The Test is probably the most beautiful of Hampshire's many lovely chalkland rivers. Its habit is not to flow as a single stream but to divide into many shining streamlets which thread their way across the broad water meadows.

Rising near Ash, it flows past the villages of Overton and Whitchurch, before bearing south to flow through Stockbridge and past Romsey to its mouth at the head of Southampton Water.

EXPLORING THE TEST
The Test Way is a 45-mile (72.4-km) trail from Inkpen Beacon to Totton, but it only actually follows the river south of Longparish. The best place to see the delightful character of the river without actually walking along it is below Stockbridge. Here roads run on both sides of the river, passing through its tranquil water meadows and over the numerous bridges that span its streams.

Ever popular with anglers, the Test flows broad and clear at Horsebridge

A Meander Around Mottisfont

A short enjoyable stroll within National Trust woodland, through the lush water meadows of the River Dun and across well-defined farmland paths. The main attractions are Mottisfont Abbey and its rose gardens, particularly beautiful and fragrant in June.

Time: 2 hours. Distance: 3 miles (4.8km).
Location: 4 miles (6.4km) northwest of Romsey.
Start: Park at Spearywell Wood National Trust car park on the B3084. (OS grid ref: SU316277.)
OS Map: Explorer 131 (Romsey, Andover & The Test Valley) 1:25,000.
See Key to Walks on page 121.

ROUTE DIRECTIONS

From the car park, pass beside the left-hand barrier and enter the predominantly coniferous woodland. Keep to the main path, then as the path bears right, turn left at the National Trust concrete waymarker and bear right through the edge of the woodland. At a crossing of paths, bear left, then almost immediately right keeping close to the wodland fringe. As the woodland thins take a path to the left which crosses a footbridge into a field. Bear slightly right on a defined path across the field to a kissing gate. Turn right beside a barrier, then turn immediately left through the woodland fringe to a stile.

Proceed on the narrow path along the edge of pasture, then beside a copse, shortly crossing a footbridge and passing beneath a railway bridge. Continue to a footbridge over the River Dun and go through the arrowed kissing gate before it on your left to enter a water meadow.

Follow the defined path through grassland (this part of the walk can be wet and boggy in places), parallel to telegraph poles, and cross two small footbridges before reaching a stile, the third footbridge and a further stile on the field edge. Head straight across the next field, over a stile and continue through grassy scrubland on a narrow path, eventually passing in front of an isolated thatched cottage.

Join its unmetalled driveway, pass through two

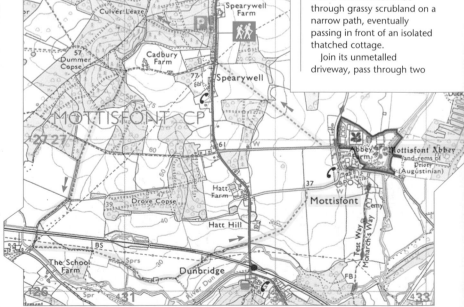

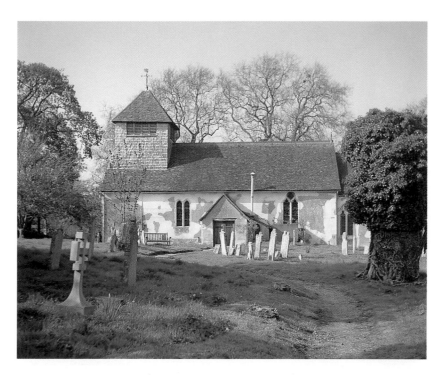

gates and soon go over a railway crossing via stiles (taking great care), and in 270 yards (246 metres) reach the B3084 at Dunbridge beyond a further gate. Go through the arrowed gap opposite and head gently uphill across the centre of a large field. Bear left behind some trees, then in a few yards rejoin the established path that bears right towards a lone tree on the edge of the field .

On reaching a narrow lane turn right and in a quarter of a mile (0.4km) enter **Mottisfont** village. At the T-junction and with Mottisfont Post Office Tea Rooms (good summer teas) on your right, bear left through the village, and turn left into Bengers Lane opposite private entrance gates to the Abbey. (Turn right at T-junction for the entrance to **Mottisfont**

Abbey and Gardens (NT) a quarter of a mile/0.4km).

In 100 yards (91 metres), climb the waymarked stile on the right and proceed diagonally left on a worn path across a field. Cut through the edge of a copse, cross a footbridge, and maintain direction through a further field to pass beside double wooden gates on to the B3084. Turn right back to the car park.

POINTS OF INTEREST

Mottisfont

The River Test, one of the finest trout-fishing rivers in the south of England, runs through this quiet village of attractive houses and cottages. The tiny Church of St Andrew boasts more 15th-century stained glass than in any other Hampshire church, including a Crucifixion in the east window, which is said to

Wooden shingles adorn the church tower at Mottisfont

have come from a ruined chapel in Basingstoke

Mottisfont Abbey and Gardens

Set picturesquely by the Test, Mottisfont Abbey is an 18th-century house adapted from a 12th-century priory. The north front shows its medieval church origins quite clearly, and the monks' 'cellarium' is virtually complete. The curious drawing-room was designed by Rex Whistler, with its walls and ceiling decorated with *trompe l'oeil* paintings. Of particular interest here are the splendid walled gardens which house the National Collection of historic roses. In June the air is heady with their fragrant perfumes.

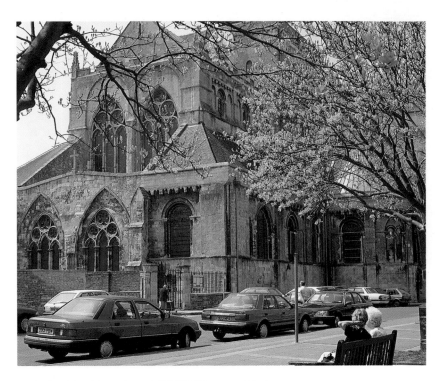

THE £100 ABBEY
Romsey Abbey survived the
Dissolution of the Benedictine
nunnery to which it was
attached because it was
purchased by the people of
Romsey who, until then, had
worshipped under sufferance
in the north transept. We
must be eternally grateful to
those Tudor townsfolk who
raised the £100 to buy it,
since not only Hampshire but
all England would be the
poorer without this wonderful
parish church.

ROMSEY Map ref SU3521
This small town on the River Test is dominated by its
superlative Abbey Church of 1120–70, a magnificently
strong Norman building with a low square tower,
massive walls, a splendid south doorway and an interior
of great beauty for which the visitor is strangely
unprepared. It contains two remarkable Saxon stone
carvings from earlier churches on the site. Lord
Mountbatten is buried in the abbey.

Romsey is an attractive place with many unobtrusively
pleasing streets of Georgian and later houses. It centres
on spacious Market Place, with a statue of Lord
Palmerston, the Victorian statesman, in the middle. The
13th-century King John's House is said to be where that
monarch's daughter lived before she married the Scottish
king. There is a lovely park beside the River Test.

Across the river are the gates of Broadlands, a fine
Palladian mansion with a splendid 18th-century portico,
set in a landscaped park. Once the home of Lord
Palmerston, more recently of Lord Mountbatten and
now of Lord Romsey, it houses exhibitions on
Mountbatten's life and a spectacular Mountbatten audio-
visual presentation in the stable block. The house
contains many fine works of art including several Van
Dycks and *The Iron Forge* by Joseph Wright of Derby.
Furniture by Ince and Mayhew was made specifically for
the house.

STOCKBRIDGE   Map ref SU3535

Lying in the broad Test valley, spanning that many-streamed river, Stockbridge consists of a wide street with open views eastwards to the hills. It feels as if it should be the main thoroughfare of a sizeable town, but it is not, and behind the elegant façades, the antique and general shops, the cafés and the hotels are the water meadows of the River Test, so beloved of anglers – some of its streamlets, teeming with trout, flow under and alongside the main street. The most prestigious of angling clubs, The Houghton, has its headquarters at the Grosvenor Hotel, Stockbridge's most impressive building, with a great porch that juts out into the street.

Stockbridge Common Marsh is ancient land in the care of the National Trust, as is the open Stockbridge Down where there is a Bronze-Age cemetery consisting of 15 round barrows. At Houghton in the Test valley near by is the Hampshire Hydroponicum, featuring plants grown in nutrient-rich water as well as more conventional riverside gardens.

WHITCHURCH   Map ref SU4648

This little town occupies an ancient site at an important crossroads on the upper reaches of the River Test (see Walk on page 28). The church, rebuilt in 1866, contains a rare Saxon tombstone, and may stand on the site of a Saxon minster. During the coaching era it bristled with inns, being the first overnight coach stop out of London, at the crossroads of the London–Exeter road and the road heading north to Newbury and Oxford. The White Hart Hotel has survived, though the other inns have now vanished.

Whitchurch is famed for having the last working silk mill in southern England, now powered by electricity, although the waterwheel has been fully restored. There is a costume exhibition and shop.

FISHING THE TEST (OR NOT!)

The River Test is world-famous for its trout fishing, which has become one of the most exclusive leisure pursuits in the country. Fishing above and below Stockbridge is controlled by two famous – and expensive – clubs, which were founded in the early 19th century and now have waiting lists for membership. The Leckford Club fishes above the village and the prestigious Houghton Club fishes the ten-mile stretch below the Leckford water.

Whitchurch's working silk mill by the river is well worth a visit

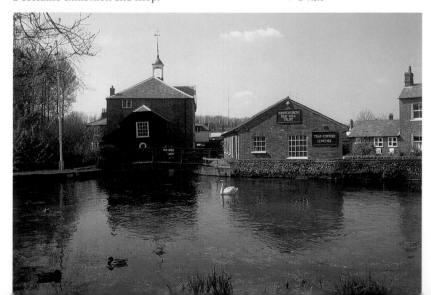

Through the Infant Test Valley

A peaceful ramble from the old coaching town of Whitchurch through the picturesque Test Valley, close to the source of Hampshire's finest chalk stream. A gentle walk on well waymarked paths.

Time: 3 hours. Distance: 5 miles (8 km).
Location: 6 miles (9.7km) northeast of Andover.
Start: Park in the Test Road car park, off Winchester Road in Whitchurch. (OS grid ref: SU464479.)
OS Map: Explorer 144 (Basingstoke, Alton & Whitchurch) 1:25,000.
See Key to Walks on page 121.

ROUTE DIRECTIONS

From the car park in **Whitchurch** walk to the junction with Winchester Road, turn left for Whitchurch Silk Mill, otherwise turn right to the main junction in the village centre. Cross straight over to follow Newbury Street past the White Hart, uphill out of the village. In a quarter of a mile (0.4km) turn right into Dances Lane, then keep left past the Police Station to

reach a turning circle.

Go ahead to cross a stile by a gate, then follow the right-hand edge of pasture to a stile in the left-hand corner, then turn left over another stile by the railway embankment. Pass beneath the railway, climb a stile on your right and follow the path around the right-hand edge of a large field to a stile and lane.

Turn right, pass the driveway to Woodlings

Vineyard, then in 150 yards (137 metres), turn right on to a green lane. Cross a bridge over the railway and gently descend, bearing left round a paddock and through a kissing gate on to the drive to Wells-in-the-Field Farm. Turn right to the B3400.

Cross over and turn left along the footway into the hamlet of **Freefolk.** In half a mile (0.8km) at the end of a row of thatched cottages turn right on to a tarmac drive, waymarked '**St Nicholas Church**' (turn left to visit St Mary's Church and note the entrance to Laverstoke Park). Cross the River Test, pass the church and Batt's Cottage and gradually climb uphill on a tree-lined track.

As the track bears left, veer right on to an arrowed path across a stile beside a field entrance. Ignore the track to the left and proceed ahead on a defined path along the top of the field with woods to the left. Eventually go through a gap in the corner, turn almost immediately right over a stile into along narrrow field.

Walk to the left along the

Almshouses at Freefolk

field edge, with **Bere Mill** visible beside the Test in the valley below, and soon proceed downhill across the pasture into the base of the valley. Ignore the stile in the left corner to reach a stile in the right-hand corner of the field. Keep to the path along the base of the hill at the valley edge, with lush water meadow to your right.

Climb a stile and follow the path along the right-hand edge of three fields, close to the River Test, eventually reaching a junction of paths by Town Mill. Bear right across the footbridge in front of the mill, then follow the track to the right of Town Mill House and alongside the river to the B3400. Turn left along the footway into Whitchurch, bearing left in the centre back to the car park.

POINTS OF INTEREST

Whitchurch

This small town developed after a market and borough were established here in the 13th century, and later grew to become an important coaching town.

Industry developed in the form of four mills which utilised the waters of the River Test to provide power. Among these were two flour mills, one of them being Town Mill.

Situated on Frog Island on the river and built in around 1800, Whitchurch Silk Mill is the last working silk mill in the south of England. It is now open to the public and visitors can see the historic looms, restored waterwheel and gardens, and there is also a shop. Teas and light lunches are available.

Freefolk

Henri Portal, a Huguenot refugee from France, established a paper mill on the Test in 1712, later moving to a mill in Laverstoke, where he started making a new watermarked banknote for the Bank of England in 1724.

The small hamlet of Freefolk housed the workers for the paper mill. The present mill is in nearby Overton and still produces banknote paper. The Portal family lived in Laverstoke Park

St Nicholas Church

Dating from the 15th century, this delightful little church was splendidly restored in 1703. The classical reredos survive and a fine 15th-century wooden screen forms the front of a family pew.

Bere Mill

This picturesque weather-boarded mill, which straddles the River Test, was where Henri Portal first established his paper-making industry in the 18th century.

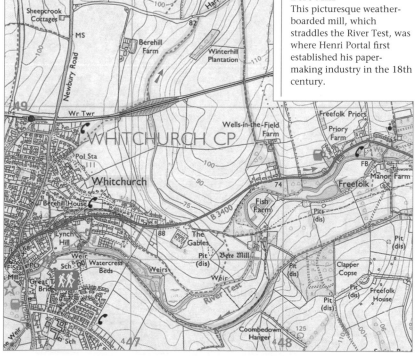

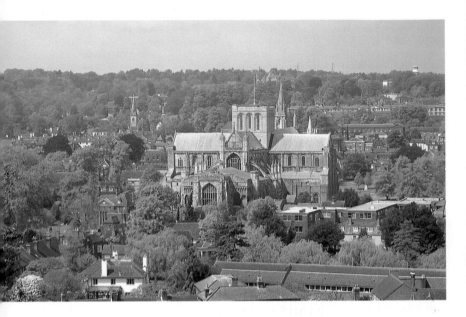

Seen from St Giles' Hill, the cathedral rises majestically from the centre of Winchester

RAIN ON ST SWITHUN'S DAY
The legend of rainy weather associated with St Swithun's Day stems from the following tale: the saint was so holy that he asked to be buried outside the cathedral, as befitted a humble servant of God. His wishes were honoured, but later his remains were translated inside the building to a sumptuous shrine, whereupon it rained heavily for 40 days, a sign of the saint's displeasure. Ever since, if it rains on St Swithun's Day, it is said that we are in for another 40 wet days.

WINCHESTER   Map ref SU4829

Physically, Winchester is relatively small. Spiritually, emotionally and historically it is large indeed. It was founded shortly before the Romans came, at an important crossing point of the River Itchen. A glance at a map shows how Roman roads radiate from the city like the spokes of a wheel, and certainly Roman Winchester – *Venta Belgarum* – was as important as this road pattern suggests. Winchester declined when the Romans left, so that when the shires were being created in the 8th century, it did not give its name to the new county, but within a century the situation had been reversed and 'Vintanceastir', as Bede called it, was again ascendant. Alfred the Great made it capital of the West Saxons in AD 871 – Hamo Thorneycroft's magnificent statue of him stands in Broadway – and Winchester remained the capital of Wessex and, in a sense, of England, well into Norman times.

The city's prestige began to dwindle once the Treasury moved to London, but the aura of past greatness still lingers and it has been said that its High Street has 'a greater wealth of historical associations than any other street in England'. Here you will find the glorious Buttercross, the former Guildhall (now a bank), with its big overhanging City Clock and statue of Queen Anne, ancient Godbegot House and the imposing 14th-century Westgate. Winchester Castle, where Henry III and Henry VIII's elder brother, Arthur, were born, was destroyed during the Civil War and only the 13th-century Great Hall remains. The top of a great round table which hangs on the west wall has been associated with King Arthur, but is probably Tudor .

The great cathedral does not dominate the city, but sits long and low among the trees and lawns of its lovely close. The present solid Norman building was begun in 1097 by Bishop Wakelin on a floating foundation of great logs, for the site was half swamp. In the 14th century Bishop William of Wykeham transformed it into what we see today, replacing the flat roof with great ribs and mouldings, adding clustered columns around the original piers and introduced spacious, elegant fan vaulting. The cathedral is dedicated to St Swithun (died AD 862), who was bishop here, and his tomb lies in the cathedral. Also here is the tomb of the notorious William II (Rufus) and a plain slab to the novelist, Jane Austen, who died near by in College Street in 1817. The famous cathedral library contains copies of the Winchester Bible and Bede's *Ecclesiastical History*.

The cathedral close contains part of the priory destroyed by Henry VIII's officers, while near by lie the ruins of the enormous Bishops' Palace, Wolvesey, largely demolished in 1800. The buildings of Winchester College, England's oldest public school, founded in 1387, lie at the end of College Street. To the south, overlooking the Itchen, is the beautiful Hospital of St Cross – surely the most picturesque almshouses in England, dating from the 12th century.

Winchester is not all history, but is a living city, with excellent shopping, many fascinating museums and a lively arts scene. (See Car Tour on page 32.)

DIVER BILL
The foundations of Winchester Cathedral, a floating platform of logs, bore up their load for 800 years, but by 1905 it was apparent that they could no longer stand the strain. The foundations were rotten and the cathedral was sinking into the swamp. It was impossible to excavate and underpin the structure, but the cathedral was saved from collapse by the work of a diver, William Walker, who, between 1906 and 1912, removed the rotten foundations by hand and replaced them with cement. A statue to him stands in a prominent place in the building he rescued.

Thorneycroft's fine statue of King Alfred gazes down the High Street

Winchester, Test Valley and the Chalk Uplands

This tour of about 55 miles (88.5km) starts at Winchester, the county town and England's ancient capital. It passes through the lush green valley of the River Test, homely villages of brick, thatch and timber, and encompasses the high chalklands of central and western Hampshire.

ROUTE DIRECTIONS

See Key to Car Tours on page 120.
Head west out of Winchester following signs to Romsey. Pass the hospital and turn right at the roundabout, signed 'Salisbury'. Take the first turning left into Sarum Road. Continue to **Farley Mount Country Park**, go over the crossroads on the high chalk hills, along the line of a Roman road. Pass the Country Park car parks, turn right at the junction going down the slope of Beacon Hill to Ashley. At a T-junction, turn left into King's Somborne, grouped around a village green overlooked by its large church.

In King's Somborne turn right, then left on to the A3057. Turn right on to the unclassified road, signed 'Horsebridge, Houghton'. Turn right in Horsebridge, signed 'Houghton', pass the mill and cross the many mill streams and streamlets of the Test to the mill in Houghton. Follow the road to the left, and keep straight on heading south down the Test meadows to Mottisfont.
Mottisfont Abbey, a former Augustinian priory, has restricted opening but the

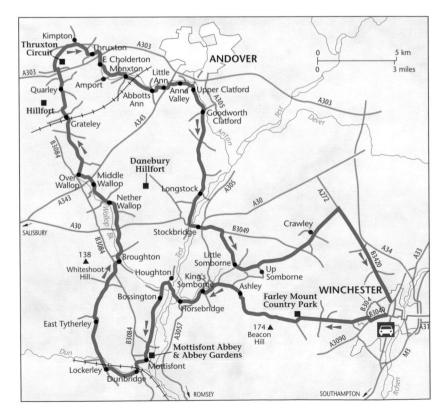

riverside **Mottisfont Abbey Gardens** (NT) are at their peak in June. Where the road bears left in the village, turn right into Hatt Lane and follow this single-track road to a T-junction. Turn left on to the B3084 to cross the level crossing at Dunbridge Station. Turn right at the Mill Arms on to the unclassified road, signed 'Lockerley'.

Turn right at the green in Lockerley, go under the railway bridge and keep straight ahead to cross the River Dun. Continue for 2 miles (3.2km) into East Tytherley and then turn right for Broughton. Continue for another 2 miles (3.2km), turn left on to the B3084 and then turn right into Broughton, a pleasing village set on either side of the Wallop Brook.

Turn left in Broughton, signed 'Middle Wallop' and follow the lane to the A30. Cross over to reach Nether Wallop, another delightful village beside Wallop Brook. Continue to Middle Wallop, then cross the A343 on to the B3084 into Over Wallop. Turn right by the war memorial into King Lane and continue past Sunnyside Farm, over a crossroads and under the railway to Grateley, an unpretentious village, with a remarkable 12th-century church.

Turn left through Grateley and then right, signed 'The Church'. Turn left, then right, running briefly along the Old Sarum–Silchester Roman road, the Portway. Bear left with the road and continue through Quarley. Go under the A303 and turn left, then almost immediately right, signed 'Kimpton'. Pass Thruxton motor racing circuit on your right. Turn right at the junction passing tiny, picturesque Kimpton (just to your left off the road). Turn right and right again into Thruxton. Follow

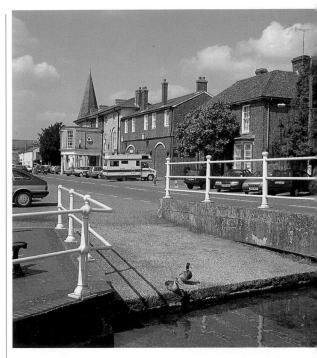

the road to the left and go under the A303. Turn left at Amport to the crossroads at the charming village of Monxton. Go straight over and across the railway to Abbotts Ann, an attractive village that was founded in 50 BC, and later granted to Hyde Abbey.

In Abbotts Ann turn right and then left beside the 'Eagle'. Continue past the church and follow the road to the right and left to Little Ann. Turn left along the A343 for a quarter of a mile (0.4km) and then right, signed 'Anna Valley, the Clatfords'. Continue to Upper Clatford, following the valley of the River Anton confluence with the Test. Carry straight on to Goodworth Clatford. In about 1¼ miles (2km) go over a crossroads and continue to Longstock, another pretty village of thatched cottages. Famous **Danebury Hillfort**

Anglers like to congregate at Stockbridge's Grosvenor Hotel

lies up on the chalk plateau to the west – detour to it by turning first right after Longstock and right again.

Continue down the Test Valley to the A30 crossroads. Turn left on to the A30 over the Test into Stockbridge, with its wide main street of gracious houses backed by the water meadows and winding streams of the river. Go over the roundabout along the B3049 for three-quarters of a mile (1.2km).

Turn right on to an unclassified road, go through Little Somborne, over the crossroads and pass the turning to Up Somborne on the right. Cross the B3049 to Crawley, a picturesque village with a duck pond. Continue and turn right on to the A272, yet another Roman road, and return to Winchester.

Winchester and the Chalk Uplands

✔ **Checklist**

Leisure Information
Places of Interest
Shopping
The Performing Arts
Sports, Activities
and the Outdoors
Annual Events and Customs

Leisure Information

TOURIST INFORMATION CENTRES

Andover
Town Mill House, Bridge Street. Tel: 01264 324320.
Romsey
1 Latimer Street. Tel: 01794 512987.
Winchester
The Guildhall, The Broadway. Tel: 01962 840500.

OTHER INFORMATION

English Heritage
Eastgate Court, 195–205 High Street, Guildford, Surrey. Tel: 01483 252000.
www.english-heritage.org.uk
Hampshire and Isle of Wight Wildlife Trust
8 Romsey Road, Eastleigh. Tel: 02380 613636.
National Trust
Southern Region, Polesden Lacey, Dorking, Surrey. Tel: 01372 453401.
www.nationaltrust.org.uk
Environment Agency
Southern Region, Guildbourne House, Chatsworth Road, Worthing, Sussex. Tel: 01903 832000.
Parking
Winchester has a park-and-ride service which is ideal for visitors coming from the M3, A31 or the A34. There are car parks at St Catherine's and Barfield; buses run every 10–15 minutes.

ORDNANCE SURVEY MAPS

Landranger 1:50,000. Sheet numbers: 174, 185.

Places of Interest

There will be an admission charge at the following places of interest unless otherwise stated.
Andover Museum and Museum of The Iron Age
6 Church Close. Tel: 01264 366283. Open all year, most days.
Avington Park
Tel: 01962 779260. Limited opening hours.
Broadlands
Romsey. Tel: 01794 505010. Open early Jun–Sep, daily.
Danebury Ring
Tel: 01962 846034/860948. Open all year. Free.
Great Hall
off High Street, Winchester. Tel: 01962 846476. Open all year, most days. Free.
Guildhall Gallery
The Broadway, Winchester. Tel: 01962 848289. Open all year, daily. Free.

Gurkha Museum
Peninsula Barracks, Romsey Road, Winchester. Tel: 01962 842832. Open all year, most days.
The Hampshire Hydroponicum
Houghton, Stockbridge. Tel: 01264 810912. Open Mar–Sep, most days.
The Sir Harold Hillier Gardens and Arboretum
Jermyns Lane, Ampfield. Tel: 01794 368787. Open all year most days.
The Hawk Conservancy
Weyhill, near Andover. Tel: 01264 772252. Open late Feb–early Nov.
Highclere Castle
Tel: 01635 253210. Open Jul–Sep, most days.
Hinton Ampner
Off A272, 1 mile (1.6km) west of Bramdean. Tel: 01962 771305. Open Apr–Sep, limited opening.
Hospital of St Cross
Winchester. Tel: 01962 851375. Open all year, most days.
King John's House
Church Street, Romsey. Tel: 01794 512200. Limited opening.
The King's Royal Hussars (PWO) Regimental Museum
Peninsula Barracks, Romsey

Road, Winchester. Tel: 01962 828541. Open daily, closed Christmas and New Year. Free.

Marwell Zoological Park
Colden Common, on B2177. Tel: 01962 777407. Over 1,000 animals, including big cats, giraffes, etc. Open all year, daily, except 25 Dec.

Mid Hants Railway
The Railway Station, Alresford. Tel: 01962 733810. The Watercress Line is open most days May–Sep; weekends Feb–Oct.

Mottisfont Abbey
Mottisfont. Tel: 01794 340757. Open: House (Whistler Room and Cellarium only) and Garden: mid-Mar to early Nov, Sat–Wed daily.

Museum of Army Flying
On A343. Middle Wallop. Tel: 01980 674421. The story of flying from the 19th century; hands-on exhibits. Open all year daily, except Christmas and New Year.

The round table in the 13th-century Great Hall of Winchester Castle

Royal Hampshire Regimental Museum and Memorial Gardens.
Serle's House, Southgate Street, Winchester. Tel: 01962 863658. Open all year, closed 2 weeks over Christmas and New Year. Free.

Sandham Memorial Chapel
Burghclere. Tel: 01635 278394. Open Apr–Oct, Wed–Sun; Mar and Nov weekends only.

Westgate Museum
High Street, Winchester. Tel: 01962 848269. Open Feb–Oct, most days.

Whitchurch Silk Mill
Winchester Street. Tel: 01256 892065. Open all year, most days.

Winchester City Mill
Bridge Sreet. Tel: 01962 870057. Open Mar, Sat and Sun, Apr–Sep, most days.

Winchester City Museum
The Square. Tel: 01962 863064/848269. Open all year, most days. Free.

Winchester College
College Street. Tel: 01962 621209. Open guided tours all year daily, except Christmas.

The following places may be of interest to visitors with children. Unless otherwise stated, there will be an admission charge.

Cholderton Rare Breeds Farm
Just west of Andover on A31. Cholderton. Tel: 01980 629438. Farm park with endangered species to be touched and fed; large collection of rabbits; pig races; pond, nature trail, adventure and toddlers playgrounds. Open late Mar–early Nov, daily.

Finkley Down Farm Park
Andover. Tel: 01264 352195. 1½ miles east, signed off the A303. Rare and not so rare breeds of farm animals; playground; pets corner. Open late Mar–early Nov, daily.

The Hawk Conservancy
Weyhill, near Andover. Tel: 01264 772252. Open late Feb–early Nov. There are flying demonstrations at 12 noon, 2pm and 3:30pm, weather permitting.

Marwell Zoological Park
Colden Common, on B2177.
Tel: 01962 777407. Over 1,000
animals including big cats,
giraffes, etc. Open all year, daily
except 25 Dec.

Mid Hants Railway
The Railway Station, Alresford.
Tel: 01962 733810. Open most
days, May– Sep; weekends
Feb–Oct.

Shopping

Alresford
Womens' Institute covered
market in Community Centre,
Thu.
There is a good selection of
shops in Broad Street, East Street
and West Street.

Andover
Open-air market in town centre,
Thu and Sat.

Romsey
Open-air market in town centre,
Fri and Sat.

Winchester
Open-air market in town centre,
Wed, Fri and Sat. Covered
antiques market in King's Walk
Mon–Sat.
Main shopping area: High
Street.

LOCAL SPECIALITIES

Crafts
Hitchcocks, 11 East Street,
Alresford. Tel: 01962 734762.

Ceramics and glass
The Candover Gallery, 22 West
Street, Alresford. Tel: 01962
733200.

Silk products
Whitchurch Silk Mill, Winchester
Street, Whitchurch. Tel: 01256
892065.

Trout
Trout can be purchased from
Avington Trout Fishery.
Tel: 01962 779312.

Watercress
Watercress can be bought from
the local farms, put money in
the honesty box and take a
bunch.

The Performing Arts

Cricklade Theatre
Charlton Road, Andover. Tel:
01264 365698.

Plaza Theatre
Winchester Road, Romsey.
Tel: 01794 523054.

Theatre Royal
Jewry Street, Winchester.
Tel: 01962 843434; box office
840440.

Sports, Activities and the Outdoors

ANGLING

Fly
Avington Trout Fishery, three
lakes and a stretch of the River
Itchen. Tel: 01962 779312.
Romsey Memorial Park. River
Test. NRA licence for salmon
fishing. Rod licence from post
offices and fishing permit from
Test Valley Borough Council
Offices, Duttons Road, Romsey.
Tel: 01794 527700.

Coarse
Anton Lakes, Andover. Rod
licence from post offices.
Information from J Eadie, Tel:
01264 351469.

COUNTRY PARKS, FORESTS AND NATURE RESERVES

Farley Mount Country Park
3 miles (4.8km) west of
Winchester near Sparsholt.

Winnal Moors Nature Reserve
Signposted from the car park at
Winchester Recreation Centre.

GOLF COURSES

Alresford
Alresford Golf Club, Cheriton
Road. Tel: 01962 733746.

Ampfield
Ampfield Par Three, Braishfield,
Winchester Road. Tel: 01794
368480.

Winchester
Royal Winchester Golf Club,
Sarum Road. Tel: 01962
852462.
Hockley Golf Club, Twyford
Down. Tel: 01962 713165.

LONG-DISTANCE FOOTPATHS

The Clarendon Way
A 24-mile (38.6-km) walk
between Winchester and
Salisbury.

The Itchen Way
A 25-mile(40.2-km) walk along
the River Itchen from Cheriton
to Southampton.

The South Downs Way
This famous long-distance
footpath/bridleway starts from
Winchester and heads east
along the Downs to end at
Eastbourne.

The Test Way
This 45-mile (72.4-km) trail runs
from Inkpen Beacon to Totton.

Wayfarer's Walk
A 70-mile (112.7-km) long-
distance path running from
Emsworth to Inkpen Beacon.

Information on the long-
distance footpaths listed above
is available from Hampshire
County Council, Arts,
Countryside and Community
Department. Tel: 01962
846002.

MOTOR RACING

Thruxton
5 miles (8km) west of Andover.
Tel: 01264 882200.

Annual Events and Customs

Alresford
Alresford Show first Sat in
September, Tichborne Park.
Street Fair, October.

Andover
Arts Festival, July.
Carnival, July.

Middle Wallop
International Air Show every
two years — check with Tourist
Information Centre

Romsey
Carnival, end July
Romsey Show at Broadlands,
September.
Firework Display at Broadlands,
Friday nearest 5 November.

Tichborne
Dole handed out 25th March
each year.

Winchester
Folk Festival, early May.
International Festival of Street
Entertainment, end June/July.

The New Forest and the Southwest Coast

The New Forest, an ancient Royal hunting forest, was created 'New' by William the Conqueror in 1079, as a preserve for the deer it was his delight to hunt. But the New Forest is not all dense woodland, as some first-time visitors expect. It consists largely of heathland, with a very rich variety of plant life and animals, including the shy New Forest deer, the famous ponies, cattle, donkeys and squirrels. Explore beyond the major

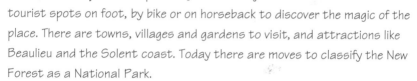

tourist spots on foot, by bike or on horseback to discover the magic of the place. There are towns, villages and gardens to visit, and attractions like Beaulieu and the Solent coast. Today there are moves to classify the New Forest as a National Park.

BEAULIEU Map ref SU3802

Visitors flock to the National Motor Museum founded at Beaulieu by Lord Montagu in 1952 in memory of his father, and now housing more than 250 vehicles including such legendary world record breakers as 'Bluebird' and 'Golden Arrow'. There are 'film star' cars, family cars from the 1930s–1950s, commercial vehicles and period street scenes. 'Wheels – The Legend of the Motor Car' takes you on a journey through a hundred years of motoring, from an Edwardian picnic to the shape of cars to come in the 21st century. The Vauxhall Driving Experience is a simulator in which you drive cars from the 1920s to modern rally cars. Costumed characters may appear during your visit to take you 'back in time' with recreations of earlier motoring history.

NEW FOREST PONIES

New Forest ponies are not wild animals – they belong to the commoners (see page 44). The number of ponies is on the decline because keeping them is not as profitable as it used to be. Moreover, since the hardy ponies who had grazed the forest for centuries were 'improved' by the Victorians, who interbred them with Arab stallions, they are not so hardy and need to eat grass. Formerly they could survive on gorse, bracken and brambles. Every autumn the commoners round up the ponies for branding and marking and several times a year ponies are sold at Beaulieu Road Station.

The old abbey gatehouse was restyled in Victorian Gothick, to become Beaulieu Palace House

Beaulieu's famous motor museum is a top visitor attraction, with vehicles dating from 1896

VISITORS FRIGHTEN GHOSTS!

All the tourist activity of recent years at Beaulieu seems to have driven the famous ghosts into hiding – for Beaulieu was formerly a much-haunted spot, and spectres, in the shape of the expelled monks, were repeatedly seen, not just at Beaulieu itself but even at Hurst Castle, where stones of the abbey had been re-used.

Alongside all this stand the ruins of Beaulieu Abbey and the gracious Palace House – the converted Abbey gatehouse. Beaulieu was *Bellus Locus*, the 'beautiful place', where King John, to atone for his many sins, founded a Cistercian monastery in 1204. The site really was beautiful, on a verdant tidal estuary beneath the bleak Beaulieu heath, and the Abbey became one of the great monastic houses of England.

At the Dissolution in 1538 the Abbey passed to Thomas Wriothesley, Earl of Southampton, who pulled most of it down – a plan of the abbey is now marked on the ground. The cloisters survived and contain a re-created monastic herb garden; the refectory became the parish church; the Domus, the lay brothers' apartments, houses an exhibition about the abbey. The Tudor house created from the 14th-century gatehouse was rebuilt in the 19th century as the present Palace House.

BREAMORE Map ref SU1517

This unspoilt village, one of the loveliest in the New Forest, has thatched cottages grouped peacefully around its village green, a scene jealously guarded from change. The little church, which dates from about 1000, has been called the most important and interesting Saxon survival in Hampshire. The 12th-century porch contains part of the Saxon rood screen, a fine piece of carving, though the figures have been damaged.

The red brick Elizabethan manor house built in 1583, but damaged by fire in the 19th century, is still a family home with collections of paintings, furniture, tapestries and porcelain. The Great Hall contains its original fireplace and there is a Victorian kitchen. The Carriage Museum in the old stable block features the last stage coach to run in England, and the fascinating Countryside Museum occupies the old farmyard.

BROCKENHURST   Map ref SU3002

Brockenhurst is a big, pleasant village in the centre of the New Forest amidst strikingly beautiful wooded country. On the northern outskirts are two of the largest and loveliest of the New Forest 'lawns', Butts Lawn and Balmer Lawn, the latter overlooked by its elegant hotel. Ponies wander at will here, unafraid of the visitors and even straying into local shops.

New Forest churches tend to stand aloof from their villages and Brockenhurst is no exception, being hidden away to the east. It is reputedly the oldest in the forest and it was certainly the only one recorded by William the Conqueror's officers in their 1086 Domesday Survey. The enormous churchyard yew that almost smothers the building has a girth of more than 20 feet (6 metres), 5 feet (1.5 metres) above ground level.

To the west of the village is the spectacular Rhinefield Ornamental Drive which was planted in the mid-19th century. It features a variety of coniferous trees, including very large redwoods. Forest walks on either side of the drive include a special 'Tall Trees Walk'. Further on is Bolderwood Drive which passes close to the famous Knightwood Oak, probably the oldest tree in the New Forest, and the deer sanctuary where platforms offer a view of deer roaming the forest.

THE MIZMAZE

The mysterious turf maze on Breamore Down is one of only two in Hampshire, the other is on St Catherine's Down, Winchester. It is a fascinating sight – a continuous turf path within a circle 80 feet (25 metres) in diameter, nothing at all like the blind-ended hedge mazes of Tudor times, such as the one at Hampton Court. Turf mazes are found only in England, and used to be constructed on village greens. They are older in design than blind-ended mazes, abound in Christian symbolism associated with the journey of the soul, and evolved on parallel lines to stone mazes found in churches on the continent.

Breamore House was used by US forces during World War II

FOREST FOLKLORE

It is not surprising that folklore lives on in the New Forest, with its wide heaths, its depths of shady woodlands and its boggy moors, for night creeps over the moorlands, straining shadows to great lengths and giving sights that are familiar and ordinary by day a weird life of their own. In the woodlands, even by day, tricks of light and shade prompt us to suspect the presence of things that defy reason. So, who should be surprised that a dragon once lived at Burley Beacon, doing unpleasant things to cattle and men and was, thankfully, finally vanquished by Sir Maurice Berkeley in Dragon Fields at Bisterne, Ringwood; or that a patented New Forest cure for any kind of sickness (*continued on next page*)

The pretty village of Burley lies west of Brockenhurst

BUCKLER'S HARD   Map ref SU4000

Two rows of terraced Georgian houses face each other across a wide open space which slopes gently down to the Beaulieu River. The area is kept free of cars and presents a peaceful rural scene today. Yet, Buckler's Hard was the shipyard which built many of the men-of-war for Nelson's fleet, including, in 1781, the famous *Agamemnon*, Nelson's favourite ship, which saw action in the battles of Copenhagen and Trafalgar. The yard was immensely busy, but overreached itself and folded in 1811. During World War II Buckler's Hard revived its ship-building tradition, for parts of one of the Mulberry Harbours for the D-Day landings were built here.

Today, pleasure craft not men-of-war ride the tranquil waters of the Beaulieu River and in summer cruises set off from the quay. The riverside walk leads to Beaulieu village, while Buckler's Hard's famous Maritime Museum displays models of many of the ships built here. Authentically reconstructed cottage interiors offer an insight into the life of 18th-century shipyard workers.

BURLEY   Map ref SU2102

Burley is an excellent centre for walks, horse-riding and mountain biking. It is an attractive village set high above the River Avon amid the bleak and gaunt heathlands of the western New Forest, where ponies and cattle roam freely. Burley Beacon is the high point of the village, reached by the gravel track from Pound Lane, and from its height the view expands westwards over the Avon Valley. Even better is the view from Castle Hill, topped

by an Iron-Age camp, at nearby Burley Street.

In the 1950s Burley had its own resident witch, Sybil Leek, but despite her 'white' tendencies local resentment at her presence, in black robes with a jackdaw on her shoulder, drove her to America. Since then Burley has specialised in witchcraft shops as well as the usual range of antiques and souvenirs.

CALSHOT AND LEPE   Map ref SU4701/SZ4498

The well-preserved remains of one of Henry VIII's chain of coastal gun-stations, built in 1539–40 against the threat of a French invasion, sits on a gravel spit jutting out into the Solent. It continued to be of military importance and now contains a reconstructed barrack room with replica 1890s furnishings and a display on the history of the fort. During both World Wars it was a Royal Naval Air Station, a base for seaplanes and flying boats, and in the 1920s and '30s the Schneider Trophy seaplane races were held here.

The beach has been designated a country park and adjoins Lepe Country Park to the west, forming a long stretch of shoreline backed by pines and cliff-top walks. The area is known for its variety of habitats – shingle beaches, reed beds, marsh and brackish ponds – which attract an extensive range of marine and bird life.

Elegant yachts and luxurious cruisers rub fenders at Buckler's Hard

(*continued from previous page*) was to wear holed stones which had been previously been exposed to the rays of the full moon for three nights? Many New Forest dwellers cursed the imp called Laurence, an unpleasant will-o'-the-wisp whose chief delight was to lure people into bogs and mires and then roar with laughter at their plight. He could change into any shape or form – like the light in the forest – and teased everyone except the first-born of a family, with merciless practical jokes.

Azaleas and rhododendrons bloom beneath the trees at Exbury Gardens

THE ELING TOLL
The causeway across the creek at Eling, as well as holding back the water, also carries the only remaining toll road in Hampshire, in operation since at least 1418. Today the tolls help to keep Eling village inviolate from rampant Southampton.

ELING Map ref SU3612

The Saxon village of Eling, on a little tidal creek off Southampton Water, was a ship-building village until the end of the 19th century and before that a small, but prestigious port from whence, in 1130, Henry I is said to have sailed to Normandy.

The creek, a sheltered little harbour for sailing craft, is crossed by a causeway with sluice gates to hold back the high tides, and in the little building on the northern shore the power of Southampton Water's famous double tides is harnessed to produce wholemeal flour. Eling Tide Mill is the only surviving tide mill regularly milling pure stoneground flour. The Domesday Book of 1086 records a mill here, but the present building dates from the 18th century. It was restored in 1980 and milling demonstrations are given, depending on the tides. You can learn more about Eling and neighbouring Totton in the heritge centre adjacent to the mill.

EXBURY Map ref SU4200

This village on the Beaulieu River is famed for its magnificent gardens featuring rhododendrons bred by Lionel de Rothschild, a banker, whose great love was gardening – and he gardened on a magnificent scale. He began to create his gardens in the 1920s from 600 acres of wooded slopes overlooking the peaceful river, dividing them into 250 acres of gardens and 350 acres of arboretum. He imported more than 1,000 varieties of rhododendron, then created 452 more by careful crossing. The mild climate of the Beaulieu River valley ensures a long flowering season, with breathtaking displays between April and June.

The rhododendrons take pride of place, but de Rothschild's collections of camellias, azaleas and magnolias contribute a great deal to the glory of an Exbury spring. Other 'gardens' include a daffodil meadow, rock garden, rose garden and water garden.

LYMINGTON Map ref SZ3295

Lymington is a pleasant town at the mouth of the Lymington River. It received its charter in 1200 and became a free port, flourishing as the closest mainland harbour to the Isle of Wight, to which ferries still run. In the Middle Ages it rivalled Southampton as a major port – and the numerous creeks around here were much frequented by smugglers well into the 18th century.

For many years Lymington's prosperity depended on the production of salt, but the trade died out and the town briefly became a fashionable bathing place. By the end of the 19th century it had developed as a sailing centre, and today the town has an excellent yacht basin and is the headquarters of two sailing clubs. There is boat building too and, as with many ports, it is famed for its inns – reputedly there were once 45.

The wide Georgian and Victorian High Street, which climbs the hill from the quay to the church, bursts into life on Saturdays when there is a vibrant 700-year-old market, with a great variety of stalls laid out along both sides of the street. Enjoy the view from the hilltop back down across the river, then take a look at the Church of St Thomas, which looks 18th century, with its jaunty white cupola and galleried interior, but is actually medieval.

To the north of Lymington is Spinners, a beautiful landscaped garden with many woodland plants.

THE SOLDIER BROTHERS' MEMORIAL
In Exbury's Church of St Catherine is a fine bronze memorial by Cecil Thomas to John and Alfred Forster, brothers who were killed in World War I. It shows a soldier's effigy lying on a tomb and was exhibited at the Royal Academy in 1924 to considerable acclaim. Impressively life-like, even down to the folds in the greatcoat, the Sam Browne belt and the lacing-up of the boots, it has an interesting history. The young sculptor was wounded in the war and while in hospital met and became firm friends with Lieutenant Alfred Forster of the Royal Scots Greys, who later died of his wounds. After the war, Lord and Lady Forster of Exbury commissioned their son's sculptor friend to design a memorial to him and his brother, who had also died.

Lymington is a centre for yacht-building on the south coast

The hamlet of Swan Green lies in some of the loveliest woodland of the New Forest

NEW FOREST COMMONERS

New Forest commoners, born of generations of New Forest folk, are independent and tough, and are as different from other 'Hampshire Hogs' as an island race cut off from the mainland. They own only tiny plots of land, for agricultural holding has been forbidden since the days when it would interfere with the King's deer. Their ponies, cattle, donkeys and geese wander freely over the heaths of the forest. Commoners' rights were clearly defined and protected in 1877 but date back to the creation of the New Forest.

LYNDHURST Map ref SU3008

The 'Capital of the New Forest' is a sizeable town, the only one within the historical confines of the forest. It was designated the New Forest's administrative centre in 1079 by William the Conqueror and is still the official seat of the ancient Court of Verderers who protect the rights of the commoners. Their Court Room and the Forestry Commission offices are both housed in the beautiful 17th-century Queen's House, and the Verderers meet every two months. All New Forest animals are under their jurisdiction, while the patrolling of the forest is in the hands of four 'Agisters' – a medieval word meaning 'collector'.

When William the Conqueror created the New Forest in 1079, it was as a preserve for deer, regarded from early times as the true sporting beasts of kings. Forest Law was severe and enforced to maintain the best possible environment for the 'beasts of the chase'. Today there are five species of deer in the forest, of which the most numerous are fallow deer. They are managed by the New Forest keepers, employed by the Forestry Commission. The New Forest Deer Sanctuary is at Bolderwood.

Lyndhurst is the home of the Museum and New Forest Visitor Centre. Its central position makes the town an ideal base for exploring the forest which still presses up close to its boundaries, so as to be only a few minutes' walk away. To the west is the picturesque thatched hamlet of Swan Green, formerly the site of an important pony fair, and Emery Down, famed for its Portuguese fireplace, which stands alone in the open air. It was constructed of cobble stones on the site of a building which was occupied by Portuguese troops during World War I and serves as a memorial to them. To the east is Bolton's Bench, an excellent starting point for walks over White Moor Heath.

Lyndhurst is a complex town of narrow streets and plenty of Victorian and Edwardian architecture. The church, on the site of two earlier ones, dates from 1860. It occupies a commanding position and contains windows by Burne-Jones and a fresco, The Parable of the Virgins, by Lord Leighton. In the churchyard lies Mrs Hargreaves, who, as the little Alice Liddell, was the model for Lewis Caroll's *Alice in Wonderland*.

Ashurst, in Langley Wood, is where you will find the New Forest Otter, Owl and Wildlife Park. Here visitors have the opportunity to view Europe's largest collection of otters, owls and other indigenous wildlife set in 25 acres of ancient woodland. On the Wildlife Walkabout look out for deer, wild boar, foxes, polecats, badgers, a lynx and hedgehogs, all in their natural surroundings.

THE WHITE HART

Of all the deer in the forest, the white buck, a rare albino form, was the most favoured. Legend has it that Henry VIII and his courtiers once chased a white buck through the forest towards Ringwood, and that he spared its life at the request of the ladies. Today the 'White Hart' appears on many an inn sign.

Pre-Raphaelite stained glass in St Michael's Church

New Forest Tracks and Paths Around Minstead

A short and easy ramble around the pretty village of Minstead on waymarked tracks and woodland paths. Thatched cottages, an historic church and the grave of Sir Arthur Conan Doyle make this an interesting walk at any time of year. Furzey Gardens are particularly attractive in spring and early summer.

Time: 2 hours. Distance: 3½ miles (5.6km).
Location: 2 miles (3.2km) northwest of Lyndhurst.
Start: Park by Minstead church.
(OS grid ref: SU281109.)
OS Map: Outdoor Leisure 22 (New Forest) 1:25,000.
See Key to Walks on page 121.

ROUTE DIRECTIONS

Go through the kissing gate to the right of **Minstead** churchyard, follow a fenced and hedged footpath between pastures and pass through a brief section of Manor Wood to reach a lane in an area called Newtown. Bear left across a footbridge beside a watersplash ford and follow the quiet lane, keeping right at a junction to pass Fleetwater Farm.

At a small green and junction near a telephone box, bear right, then in a few yards turn left with fingerpost on to a defined bridleway. Gently climb uphill on the wide holly-edged path, then on reaching a grassy area, bear right alongside the road. Turn immediately right before a post box (blue arrow) on to

a track and fork left passing a house called Skymers. At another fork, bear right and gradually descend to reach a metalled lane.

Climb a waymarked stile on your left beside the driveway to Oakleaf Cottage, and shortly drop down on the narrow path to a footbridge and stile. Proceed uphill, then just beyond a further stile, follow the yellow arrow sharp right, downhill through woodland and over a footbridge.

Follow the boarded path uphill across a boggy area, then on reaching a fork of paths, bear right with a yellow arrow go through a walk-through stile and continue to climb, eventually joining a path from the left, and enter the parking area to **Furzey Gardens**. Bear right past the entrance, then turn right down to a lane and follow it to a T-junction beside Minstead village hall.

Turn left, then take the second lane right (signed 'No access to A31') and shortly

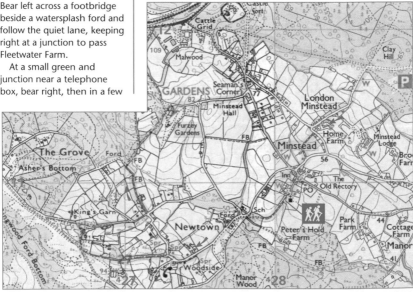

cross a bridge. In 50 yards (46 metres) take the unmarked path right on to a wide pathway through woodland. The path may become ill-defined in places, but maintain direction, eventually emerging into a clearing with a house and smallholding to your right.

Join its gravel driveway, then turn right along a lane into Minstead. Just over the top of the hill turn left into Bull Lane, then in 50 yards (45 metres) opposite Home Farm, take the arrowed path right through a kissing gate. Go through a further gate, turn left, then turn right along a metalled lane back to the village centre. At T-junction, turn left, then right, past the **Trusty Servant pub** back to the church.

The old cottage provides a charming focal point in Furzey Gardens

POINTS OF INTEREST

Minstead

Recorded in the Domesday Book as 'Mintestede', meaning 'a place where mint is grown', this pretty village is set in a maze of lanes and boasts a wealth of picture-postcard thatched cottages.

Positioned on a secluded little hill lies the Church of All Saints, which dates from the 13th century and was originally thatched. With rubble-and-daub walls and gabled windows it looks more like a row of cottages. Inside, it has several distinctive characteristics, namely an unusual triangular nave, a triple-decker pulpit, a double tier of galleries and a pew fireplace. Within the churchyard can be found a 400-year-old yew tree and among other notable graves, the grave of the best known

Minstead resident, Sir Arthur Conan Doyle, who created the character Sherlock Holmes. Conan Doyle lived at nearby Bignall Wood.

Furzey Gardens

The cottage which stands in the gardens dates from 1560 and with the gallery provides a charming venue of local arts and crafts. Eight acres of peaceful glades around the cottage are particularly beautiful in spring and early summer.

Trusty Servant Pub

The unusual 'Trusty Servant' inn sign is modelled on a picture in Winchester College. The composite creature embodies a pig for unfussiness in diet – its snout locked for secrecy – an ass for patience, a stag for swiftness and a laden hand for hard work. It is accompanied by a verse.

The Rufus Stone tells its own tale

WHERE WILLIAM RUFUS FELL

William II (Rufus), hard-bitten son of the Conqueror, loved hunting and it was in the New Forest that he died, killed by an arrow supposedly intended for a deer. The Rufus Stone at Canterton Glen is said to mark the spot, but some say it was near Bolderwood, or Stoney Cross, or Fritham. More sinister still, some question whether the king's death was an accident. At all events, his brother Henry rode straight to Winchester to be proclaimed king, while William's body was carried there on the cart of a charcoal burner whose name was Purkess. There are still Purkesses around here.

MINSTEAD   Map ref SU2811

Minstead consists of clusters of cottages amidst trees and pastures, centred on the inn and church. The latter is of curious construction having the appearance of an old house, all gables and dormers, the result of successive 'updates' by local builders who had little idea of ecclesiastical building, reflecting the unhurried days when the forest turned in on itself and knew little of the world beyond. The interior has rows of box pews and a plethora of galleries. Sir Arthur Conan Doyle (1867–1930) and his wife are buried here (see Walk on page 46).

Near by are Furzey Gardens, renowned among botanists and horticulturists, comprising eight acres of informal planting, including azaleas, rhododendrons, ferns, heathers and Chilean Fire trees. Within the garden are a Tudor cottage and a local crafts gallery. Further west is the Rufus Stone, marking the place where William II (Rufus) met his death.

RINGWOOD   Map ref SU1505

Ringwood stands on the River Avon, and anglers come from miles around for the coarse and salmon fishing of this reach. The pleasant, busy place has always been the New Forest's market town, a pleasing mix of architectural styles with modern buildings blending well with Georgian houses and older cottages.

There is a good modern shopping centre, while the attractive High Street has traditional shops including fishing tackle suppliers and a gunsmith. In West Street stands Monmouth House where the Duke of Monmouth was held after his defeat at Sedgemoor in 1685, before being sent to London for execution.

To the south of Ringwood at Crow is the New Forest Owl Sanctuary, dedicated to rehabilitating sick and wounded birds and releasing them back to the wild. Flying displays are carried out three times daily and there are lectures, videos, a picnic area and café.

ROCKBOURNE   Map ref SU1118

The village of Rockbourne, on the high chalklands west of the New Forest, is one of Hampshire's prettiest villages, nestling beside a stream in a valley bottom, but its fame rests on the Roman villa discovered by a farmer digging out a ferret in 1942 (see Walk on page 50).

Rockbourne Villa was a large courtyard type of villa, possibly part of an imperial estate, with more than 70 rooms and several bath suites. It was occupied from the mid-2nd century AD until the collapse of Roman rule in the early 5th century. Although much of it has been excavated it has to some extent been backfilled, since the site is not under cover. As well as the villa, there was a small settlement and a probable cattle enclosure on Rockbourne Down, while nearby Bokerley Dyke, a late Roman earthwork, acts as a local boundary.

The museum attached to the villa has pottery, jewellery and elaborate iron work, a large coin hoard and two Roman milestones. Found in the fabric of the villa, where they had been re-used as building material, they date from the reigns of Trajan Decius (AD 249-51) and Tetricus II (AD 272).

THE HAMPSHIRE AVON

The River Avon rises to the east of Devizes and flows southwards for 48 miles (77.2km) to the English Channel at Christchurch. It is more of a Wiltshire than a Hampshire river, and in its upper chalky reaches it is a noted trout stream, but where it flows into Hampshire past Breamore and Fordingbridge the acid soils of the New Forest change its nature and it becomes a river for coarse fishing. It forms the boundary between Hampshire and Dorset in the Ringwood area and below Ringwood is renowned for salmon. In Hampshire it is particularly rich in wildlife, and a large part is a Site of Special Scientific Interest. The waymarked Avon Valley Path follows the river for 34 miles (54.7km) from Salisbury to Christchurch.

New, golden thatch on a cottage in Rockbourne

A Ramble Around Rockbourne

A gently undulating walk that explores farm and woodland paths and pretty downland villages. Scenic Avon Valley views and a wealth of historic interest, from a Roman villa to a fortified Iron-Age camp, make this an excellent outing at any time of the year.

Time: 3½ hours. Distance: 5 miles (8km).
Location: 3 miles (4.8km) northwest of Fordingbridge.
Start: Rockbourne Village Hall.
(OS grid ref: SU114183.)
OS Map: Explorer 130 (Salisbury & Stonehenge) 1:25,000.
See Key to Walks on page 121.

ROUTE DIRECTIONS

From **Rockbourne** hall turn left along the village street, then soon turn right along a track, waymarked to **Manor Farm**. At the farm, turn right then bear left across a gravel drive and walk up a stepped path to the left of a topiary hedge to pass the entrance to **St Andrew's Church**.

Go to a footpath fingerpost and keep straight on along a narrow path behind houses. Ignore three paths on the right, cross a stile, and turn right through a gate. Walk down the right-hand field edge, then turn left at the crossing of paths at the bottom. Go through a gate and keep ahead over a stile to the right corner of a paddock. Keep right-handed through a field, a gate and further field to a stile. Turn right over a further stile into a meadow, keep to left-hand edge and follow waymarkers in front of a cottage and drop on to the driveway to Marsh Farm.

Turn left, then promptly right through a gate and keep right across a paddock to a gate. Follow waymarkers across pasture and eventually reach a lane. (To visit **Rockbourne Roman Villa** turn right.) Cross the lane on to a track, then at a crossing of tracks in a copse, bear left up the steep bank into a field.

Turn left across waymarked fields to a farm track. Turn right, then left with waymarker downhill through the edge of woodland and to the left of a house to a lane. Turn right, then almost immediately left into woodland and proceed uphill, bearing left at a junction of paths to reach a lane. Turn left, then immediately right on to a waymarked trackway between dwellings.

Follow the track to the lane at Whitsbury Common, turn right and veer right on to a defined path that soon enters Whitsbury Wood. On merging with a track bear right and on emerging from the wood keep alongside paddocks. Turn left by a bungalow, pass between paddocks, then left at a T-junction of tracks and shortly enter the churchyard to St Leonard's Church.

Leave by the gate opposite the porch and descend into **Whitsbury.** Turn right up the road. Walk through the village eventually passing the stables of Whitsbury Manor Stud and bear left past its main entrance. As the road bears right, take the waymarked path left, through a small close, a gate and down an avenue of beech trees. Keep left where it narrows, pass through two gates and head downhill through more beech trees to three further gates. Proceed across pasture towards Rockbourne church and merge with track that leads through Manor Farm back into the village.

A striking Roman floor mosaic at Rockbourne

POINTS OF INTEREST

Rockbourne

The village's one long winding street is one of the prettiest in Hampshire, lined with Tudor and Georgian houses and splendid thatched and timber-framed cottages. Those on the north side are reached across little bridges spanning a brook.

Manor Farm

An interesting complex of medieval buildings, including a 13th-century chapel, a small 14th-century house to which is attached an Elizabethan east wing, and a 15th-century barn with two magnificent waggon porches.

St Andrew's Church

Originally Norman, but changed and extended in the 13th and late 19th centuries, the church has a tiny oak shingled spire dating from 1630, an ornate porch (1893) and some fine memorials to the Coote family who resided near by.

Rockbourne Roman Villa

Discovered in 1942, these remains of a Roman villa are the largest in the area and represent a fine display of mosaics and hypocaust.

Whitsbury

Tucked amid rolling downland, this peaceful settlement boasts a fortified Iron-Age camp covering 16 acres, surrounded by a triple circle of great banks with two deep ditches. St Leonard's Church dates from 1878 and enjoys splendid views across the Avon Valley and the New Forest. Whitsbury Manor Stud is one of the most successful horse-breeding, training and racing stables in Britain, the open downland surrounding the village providing an ideal training ground for potential winners. Desert Orchid and Rhyme and Reason were both bred at the stud.

The New Forest and the Southwest Coast

Leisure Information

Places of Interest

Shopping

Sports, Activities and the Outdoors

Annual Events and Customs

✓ Checklist

Leisure Information

TOURIST INFORMATION CENTRES

Beaulieu
National Motor Museum.
Tel: 01590 612345.
Lymington
The St Barbe Building, New Street. Tel: 01590 672422.
Lyndhurst
New Forest Museum and Visitor Centre, Main Car Park. Tel: 02380 282269.
Ringwood
The Furlong. Tel: 01425 470896 (open three times a week Nov–Mar).

OTHER INFORMATION

English Heritage
Eastgate Court, 195–205 High Street, Guildford, Surrey. Tel: 01483 252000.
www.english-heritage.org.uk
Forestry Commission
Queens House, Lyndhurst. Tel: 02380 283141.
Hampshire and Isle of Wight Wildlife Trust
8 Romsey Road, Eastleigh. Tel: 02380 613636.
National Trust
Southern Region, Polesden Lacey, Dorking, Surrey. Tel: 01372 453401.
www.nationaltrust.org.uk

Environment Agency
Southern Region, Guildbourne House, Chatsworth Road, Worthing, Sussex. Tel: 01903 832000.

ORDNANCE SURVEY MAPS

Landranger 1:50,000. Sheet numbers 184, 195, 196.
Outdoor Leisure 1:25,000. Sheet number 22

Places of Interest

There will be an admission charge at the following places of interest unless otherwise stated.
Beaulieu: National Motor Museum
Beaulieu, on B3054. Tel 01590 612345. Open all year, daily except Christmas Day.
Breamore House, Countryside and Carriage Museums
near Fordingbridge. Tel: 01725 512468. Open Apr–Sep, most days.
Buckler's Hard Village and Maritime Museum
off B3054. Tel: 01590 616203. Open all year daily, except Christmas Day.
Eling Tide Mill
Eling Toll Bridge, Totton. Signposted from A35. Rare surviving tide mill, still

producing stone-ground flour. Tel: 02380 869575. Open all year, most days.
Exbury Gardens
Exbury Estate. 3 miles (4.8km) from Beaulieu, off B3054. Tel: 02380 891203. Particularly famous for rhododendrons in the early summer. Open late Feb–late Nov, daily.
Furzey Gardens
Minstead. Tel: 02380 812464. Peaceful gardens, plus cottage gallery of arts and crafts. Open all year daily, except Christmas.
Hurst Castle
Accessible on foot, or by boat from Keyhaven. Tel: 01590 642344. Open Apr–Oct, daily.
New Forest Otter, Owl & Wildlife Park
Deerleap Lane, Longdown, Ashurst, off A35. Tel: 02380 292408. Open all year, daily from 10am.
New Forest Museum & Visitor Centre
Main Car Park, High Street, Lyndhurst. Tel: 02380 283914. Open all year, daily except Christmas.
The New Forest Owl Sanctuary
Crow Lane, near Ringwood. Tel: 01425 476487. Open all year, daily.

Roman Villa
Rockbourne. Tel: 01725 518541. Open Apr–Sep, daily.

Spinners
School Lane, Boldre, off A337. Tel: 01590 673347. Open mid-Apr to mid-Sep, daily.

SPECIAL INTEREST FOR CHILDREN

The following places of interest may be of interest to visitors with children. Unless otherwise stated there will be an admission charge.

Longdown Activity Farm
Deerleap Lane, Longdown, Ashurst. Tel: 02380 293326. Working farm and children's farm. Open Easter–Oct.

New Forest Otter, Owl and Wildlife Park
Deerleap Lane, Longdown, Ashurst, off A35. Tel: 02380 292408. Open all year, daily.

The New Forest Owl Sanctuary
Crow Lane, near Ringwood. Tel: 01425 476487. Open all year, daily.

Paultons Park
Ower. Off Junc 2 M27. Tel: 01703 814455. Over 40 attractions including exciting rides, exotic birds and animals. Open mid-Mar to Oct, daily; Nov–Dec, weekends.

Shopping

Lymington
Open-air market in town centre, Sat.

Ringwood
Open-air market in town centre, Wed.

LOCAL SPECIALITIES

Cider
New Forest Cider, Littlemead, Pound Lane, Burley, near Ringwood. Tel: 01425 403589.

Pottery
Kristen Pottery, High Street. Beaulieu. Tel: 01590 612064.

Sports, Activities and the Outdoors

ANGLING

Sea
Sea fishing trips are available from Keyhaven. Tel: 01425 612896.

Fly
Turf Croft Farm, Forest Road, Burley. Tel: 01425 403743.

Coarse
Ringwood. For details contact Ringwood Tourist Information Centre.

BEACHES

Barton on Sea
Pebble and shingle beach, safe only when sea is calm.

Lepe Country Park
Near Calshot Castle. Shingle and sand beach.

Milford on Sea
Pebble beach, dangerous when sea is rough.

BOAT TRIPS

Lymington
Various boat trips are available including river cruises and trips to Yarmouth. For more details contact Puffin Cruises (on the quay at Lymington). Tel: 07850 947618.

COUNTRY PARKS AND NATURE RESERVES

Lepe Country Park and the Calshot foreshore.

CYCLING

There is plenty of cycling in the New Forest. Contact Lyndhurst Tourist Information Centre for cycle routes and bike hire.

CYCLE HIRE

Brockenhurst
New Forest Cycle Experience, The Island Shop, Brookley Road. Tel: 01590 624204.

Burley
Burley Bike Hire, The Cross. Tel: 01425 403584.

GOLF COURSES

Barton on Sea
Barton on Sea Golf Club, Milford Road. Tel: 01425 615308.

Brockenhurst
Brockenhurst Manor Golf Club, Sway Road. Tel: 01590 623332.

Dibden
Dibden Golf Centre, Main Road. Tel: 02380 207508.

Lyndhurst
Bramshaw Golf Club, The Clubhouse, Brook. Tel: 02380 813433.

HORSE-RIDING

Applemore
The Old Barn, Dale Farm, Manor Road, Applemore Hill, Dibden. Tel: 02380 843180.

SAILING

Lymington
Lymington Town Sailing Club. Tel: 01590 674514.
Royal Lymington Yacht Club. Tel: 01590 672677.

Milford on Sea
Hurst Castle Sailing Club, The Clubhouse, Keyhaven. Tel: 01590 645589.
Keyhaven Yacht Club. Tel: 01590 642165.

WAGON RIDES

Burley
Burley Wagonette Rides, Queens Head Car Park. Tel: 07000 924667.

Annual Events and Customs

Beaulieu
Boat Jumble, April.
Auto Jumble, September.
Fireworks, Fri nearest 5 November.

Brockenhurst
New Forest Show, last week July.
Carnival and fête, August Bank Hol Mon.

Fordingbridge
Carnival, July.
Fordingbridge Show, mid-July.
Fireworks, Sat nearest 5 November.

Netley Marsh
Netley Marsh Steam Rally, Fri–Sun in late July.

Ringwood
Carnival, mid-September.

The checklists give details of just some of the facilities within this guide. Further information can be obtained from Tourist Information Centres.

The Isle of Wight

The Isle of Wight is the largest island off the English Coast, separated from the mainland by the Solent. Although administratively part of Hampshire, it is a separate world, for many years isolated and forgotten, until popularised by the arrival in the mid-19th century of Queen Victoria and Prince Albert, who built Osborne House. This is an island of contrasts: the north facing the mainland; the southwest, including the famous 'Needles', battered by channel storms, and the southeast basking in a sub-tropical climate. The Isle of Wight has a timeless, old fashioned appeal which lingers on, born of its long separation from the mainland and an independent way of life; indefinable but nevertheless real, it helps explain the island's perennial popularity.

THE ISLE OF WIGHT FERRIES
Ferries take pride of place in the Isle of Wight 'experience' – an essential part of that holiday spirit. The best known services run from Portsmouth: a car ferry to Fishbourne (35 minutes) and a foot-passenger catamaran to Ryde Pier (5 minutes). The hovercraft from Southsea to Ryde Pier takes only 8 minutes, but for a more leisurely trip, try the Southampton to East Cowes car ferry – a relaxing hour-long trip; the swift hydrofoil from Southampton to Cowes takes just 20 minutes. Saving the best till last, the car ferry from Lymington to Yarmouth (30 minutes) is the most scenic and pleasurable crossing.

Leaving Cowes – the ferries are the island's lifeline

ARRETON Map ref SZ5386
The church at Arreton is one of the island's best. The original early Norman church was rebuilt in the 13th century, after the settlement of a dispute over it between the Abbeys of Quarr and Lyre (France). It contains an early 15th-century brass – now headless – to Henry Hawls, who fell at Agincourt, while in the churchyard lie all that was mortal of Oliver Cromwell's grandson, William, and the dairyman's daughter Elizabeth Wallbridge, heroine of a popular Victorian tract.

Arreton Manor (not open to the public) was rebuilt between 1595 and 1612 for Sir Humphrey Bennet and is regarded by many as the island's most beautiful historic house. It was designed on an H-plan, with a front entrance and porch dated 1639. The site is ancient – it once belonged to Alfred the Great, then to the monks of Quarr Abbey (near Ryde), and part of their farmhouse is incorporated in the Elizabethan building, said to be haunted by the ghost of a little girl who was murdered by her brother.

Near by is the Arreton Old Village Barns complex, with a craft workshop, the House of Lavender shop with themed gardens and water features, and various children's play areas.

A mile to the southeast of Arreton is Haseley Manor, one of the most interesting historic houses on the island, built in 1550. It was renovated during the 1980s and is now a superb setting for a display of fine furniture and costume which illustrates its history, from medieval times to the Victorian era. Hasely Manor also has splendid water, herb and flower gardens, a children's farm, a pottery studio, and a large collection of rural implements and historic vehicles.

The village of Arreton lies amid beautiful rolling countryside

OVER ARRETON DOWN
This short drive affords spectacular views. Leave Newport eastwards on the A3034 and turn right to Barton. Bear right at Staples and continue to Downend, where a road joins from the left. Fork left up onto Arreton Down, and at the highest point ignore the right turn and keep straight on downhill. The road then starts to climb again; turn right just before the road turns sharp left, keeping to the high ground to Brading Down, before plunging down into Brading.

Bembridge harbour has gradually reverted to marsh, but is still deep enough for small craft

VICTORIAN DEFENCES

Bembridge Down, above the town and airport, is crowned by Fort Bembridge (1862–7) the main Victorian fort for the southern Isle of Wight, while offshore four forts are visible – the remains of Victorian defences for Spithead.

MOLLY DOWNER

Tales are told in Bembridge of local witch and smuggler, Molly Downer, who cheerfully embarrassed the vicar by leaving him her cottage.

BEMBRIDGE Map ref SZ6488

Until the Victorians discovered it, Bembridge was a remote fishing village in a sheltered haven leading to Brading Quay. The Brading Harbour Improvement and Railway Company set out to reclaim the upper reaches of the haven and create a deep-water port at Bembridge, building an embankment between here and St Helens in 1878 to carry both road and rail. But Bembridge's days as a port were already numbered. The ferry service to the mainland lasted only from 1882–8 as the new harbour suffered from silting. The railway survived through the first half of the 20th century. There are pleasant walks inland, over the reclaimed haven, now marshy meadows, to ancient Brading.

Bembridge is a popular sailing centre and a quiet resort. At Bembridge Point is the famous Pilot Boat Inn, built in the shape of a boat, and the lifeboat station near by houses displays on its modern unsinkable craft. It is a busy lifeboat – and the danger of the waters round the Isle of Wight can be fully appreciated by a visit to the Shipwreck Centre and Maritime Museum. Bembridge Windmill, half a mile (0.8km) south, dates from 1700.

BRADING Map ref SZ6087

In Roman times Bembridge Down was a separate island and Brading faced it across a tidal channel. It was here in about AD 300 that the Romans built the now-famous villa, one of the best in Britain, and it remained occupied until the 5th century (see Walk on page 58).

In 1338 an embankment was built at Yar Bridge, creating a harbour connecting Bembridge Down with the rest of the Isle of Wight. Brading became an important port, but the harbour suffered from increased silting. It was reclaimed in 1878–80 and is now an area of marshy meadows, a favourite breeding ground for birds.

The Wax Museum illustrates famous and infamous characters who populated 2,000 years of Isle of Wight history, complete with sound, light and animation. The town also has the Lilliput Museum of Antique Dolls and Toys and Animal World, displaying birds and reptiles in colourful dioramas. Morton Manor, rebuilt in 1680, claims to possess the island's most beautiful gardens and has a vineyard producing some of the island's best wines.

The ancient Church of St Mary is said to mark the spot where St Wilfred converted the island to Christianity. It has a Norman nave, a 13th-century tower and a chapel containing tombs of the important Oglander family. To the northwest of Brading is Nunwell House, a 17th-century mansion and seat of the Oglanders from the Norman conquest till 1980. Charles I spent his last night on the island here.

THE OGLANDER FAMILY

The Oglanders could be regarded as the island's 'royal family'. The founder of the family, Roger de Orglandes, came to England with William the Conqueror and his family had established their seat at Nunwell by the time Henry I came to the throne. For 800 years the Oglanders played a very important part in the affairs of the Isle of Wight. Sir John Oglander, who lived during the time of Cromwell, wrote a celebrated history of the island, in which he described Brading as 'the awntientest towne in owre Island'.

Brading's Wax Museum can boast 366-day opening throughout the year

Brading Down

From historic Brading, this walk explores the parkland of Nunwell House and the ancient chalk grassland on Brading Down, affording views north across the Solent and south over Sandown Bay. Along the way are two museums and manor houses and a Roman villa. Good, waymarked paths and one steep descent.

Time: 2 hours (longer if visiting attractions along the way).
Distance: 5 miles (8km).
Location: 2 miles (3.2km) north of Sandown.
Start: Park in Brading Town Car Park on A3055, near the church. (OS grid ref: SZ606874.)
OS Map: Outdoor Leisure 29 (Isle of Wight) 1:25,000.
See Key to Walks on page 121.

ROUTE DIRECTIONS

From the car park, turn left along the main street in **Brading,** passing the church,

the Old Town Hall and the **Wax Museum** before turning right beside **Lilliput Toy and Doll Museum** into

Cross Street. At a T-junction, bear right along a wide metalled path leading to a road. Turn left, pass the entrance to **Nunwell House**, then in 50 yards (46 metres) climb the waymarked stile on your left, signed 'Nunwell Farm'. Cross a further stile, then follow a line of oak trees to a stile near New Farm.

Proceed ahead, walk alongside a hedge, then at fingerpost bear half-right across pasture to an arrowed tree, and shortly cross a stile by a large oak tree. Continue to a waymarked stile and farm road. Turn left towards Nunwell Farm taking the arrowed path right alongside farm buildings (can be muddy) for Brading Down. Pass through a gate and proceed uphill with blue arrow on worn track to two metal gates. Keep to the grassy track along the right-hand edge of pasture – Bembridge Trail – to a further

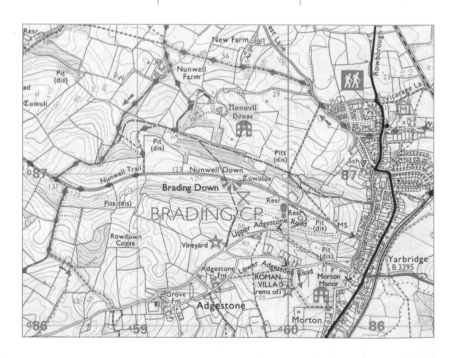

gate and bear right around the field edge to a wooden gate and road on top of Brading Down.

Turn left along the grass verge, then in 75 yards (67.5 metres) cross over to take the narrow hedged path, signposted 'Alverstone'. Descend steeply with splendid views and in a quarter of a mile (0.4km) cross the stile in the left-hand hedgerow into pasture. Keep right to a stile, climb a further arrowed stile beside a gate on your right and bear diagonally left uphill across a field to a stile. Proceed on a defined path towards a house and cross a stile on to a lane.

Turn left, pass Grove Farm, then in a quarter of a mile (0.4km) turn right along a lane passing Well House. Shortly, at a T-junction turn left, pass Adgestone Farm, then in 30 yards (27 metres) cross the waymarked stile on the right, signed 'Roman Villa'. Head straight across an open field to a junction of paths in the field corner by a lane. Turn right, pass in front of the **Roman Villa**, follow its driveway, bearing left to a lane.

Turn left and soon turn left again into Morton Manor Road to pass the entrance to **Morton Manor**. At a junction bear left into The Mall, following the footway uphill, and proceed for half a mile (0.8km) to reach Brading High Street, which leads back to the church and car park.

Imposing iron gates lead to Nunwell House, visited by Henry VIII and Charles I

POINTS OF INTEREST

Brading

This inland village was a thriving port before the River Yar was dammed at St Helens in 1877 and the estuary drained, leaving the quayside high and dry. The 12th-century Church of St Mary has an unusual porch-tower, and is also noted for wooden Oglander monuments. The adjacent Old Town Hall preserves stocks and a whipping post.

Wax Museum

Housed partly within the half-timbered Rectory Mansion dating from 1228 – the oldest house on the island – this fascinating museum portrays island, national and international history from Roman times to the present day.

Lilliput Toy and Doll Museum

This private collection contains one of the finest collections of dolls in Britain. There are over 2,000 exhibits, ranging in age from 2,000 BC to 1945.

Nunwell House

Set in beautiful gardens, Nunwell is an impressive, lived-in and much-loved house where Charles I spent his last night of freedom.

Brading Roman Villa

The villa is believed to have been the centre of a rich and prosperous farming estate with fine mosaic floors, painted walls and luxury objects.

Morton Manor

The manor dates back to 1249, but was rebuilt in 1680 with further changes during the Georgian period. The main attractions here

REFUGE DENIED
In 1647 Charles I sought
refuge from the governor of
Carisbrooke Castle, Colonel
Hammond, who, instead of
aiding his flight to France,
imprisoned him and sent him
from Carisbrooke to the
scaffold in 1648. Charles'
youngest children, Princess
Elizabeth and Prince Henry,
were imprisoned at
Carisbrooke in 1650 and the
little princess died of fever
within a month. The boy
survived and was later allowed
to go abroad.

CALBOURNE Map ref SZ4286

Calbourne is tucked under the downs, an unspoilt little
place on the Caul Burn with a village green, a Norman
and 13th-century church and pretty stone cottages (see
Walk on page 66). The best of these are in Barrington
Row, which everyone calls 'Winkle Street' (because it is
so small); these low thatched cottages tucked away at the
back of the village face the diminutive Caul Burn.

The Caul Burn formerly powered five watermills, and
the last surviving, Calbourne Mill, first mentioned in
1299, is still in working order; there is an attached rural
life museum with all manner of interesting old
appliances. West of Calbourne is Chessell Pottery, a
pottery housed in a large old barn, while to the east is
historic Swainstone House, now a hotel, renovated after
being burnt out in an air raid in 1941. It was named after
Swein, the 8th- to 9th-century Danish leader, and later
belonged to the Bishop of Winchester. The attached
13th-century chapel survived intact.

CARISBROOKE Map ref SZ4888

Carisbrooke, once the capital of the Isle of Wight, stands
some way inland above the Medina River and is
overlooked by its castle, one of England's most
impressive. High Street is pleasant, and narrow Castle
Street leads up from an old ford and streamside footpath
to the castle. Beautiful St Mary's Church, with its lofty
15th-century tower, was the church of a priory dissolved
as long ago as 1415.

To many, though, Carisbrooke is its castle and the
castle is Carisbrooke. It is a big well-preserved Norman
fortress on the site of a Roman fort. The oldest part is the
keep and the surviving sections of curtain walls which
were thrown up around it in the 12th century. At the
end of the 16th century, because of the use of bigger
cannons, these walls were strengthened. You need a
head for heights to walk the ramparts, but you will be
rewarded with excellent views of the interior of the
castle and the surrounding countryside. One of the
greatest attractions is the well, 161 feet (49 metres) deep
with a 16th-century wheel designed to bring up the
water. It is worked today by a donkey but used to be
turned by prisoners. The castle also houses the
fascinating Isle of Wight Museum.

*Charles I was held prisoner
in Carisbrooke Castle in
1647, when an attempt to
escape by squeezing
through the window bars
ended in undignified failure*

COWES Map ref SZ4996

Cowes is two distinctly different places, divided by the River Medina. On the west bank is the sailing capital of Britain, on the east a residential and industrial place beyond which is Osborne House, former Royal residence of Queen Victoria. In fact, Queen Victoria can be said to have 'discovered' the Isle of Wight, when in the 1840s she and Prince Albert made Osborne House their home. Where Royalty led others followed and the island, remote until then, was thronged by a stream of tourists, which has continued ever since.

West Cowes, home of the Royal Yacht Squadron, has an attractive winding High Street and a good array of shops. Ships and boats of all sorts can be watched from the Victoria Parade. The first Cowes Regatta took place between naval vessels in 1776, and the yacht club was founded in 1815 with its headquarters at Cowes Castle, one of King Henry VIII's fortifications. There have always been Royal yachtsmen – Edward VII, George V, Prince Philip and Prince Edward – and during 'Cowes Week' in August the little town is alive with the great and the good of the yachting fraternity. Cowes has a Maritime Museum and the Sir Max Aitken Museum, which has a display of nautical instruments, paintings and artefacts.

Osborne House (English Heritage) was designed by Prince Albert and Thomas Cubitt in the style of an Italian villa. Queen Victoria died here in 1901 and Edward VII gave it to the nation. The state and private apartments are furnished as in Victoria's time and in the beautiful grounds is the Swiss Cottage, the royal children's playhouse. Nearby Barton is a much older place with a medieval manor house rebuilt by Prince Albert as an experimental farm. Today its lovely gardens are open to the public, as is the award-winning vineyard.

THE ROYAL YACHT SQUADRON

Probably the most prestigious yachting club in the world, the Royal Yacht Squadron was founded as the Yacht Club in 1815 with 42 members 'of good social standing' who wore 'a common blue jacket and white trousers'. This uniform was described as 'far from unbecoming to such as are not too square in the stern'. Membership included virtually half the British aristocracy, including the Prince Regent, and the club became 'Royal' in 1820 when he ascended the throne as George IV. It was renamed the Royal Yacht Squadron in 1833 by his brother, William IV. In 1856 Cowes Castle became the Squadron's headquarters and the 22 brass guns from the *Royal Adelaide*, William IV's yacht, were positioned in front of the castle to start races and salute victorious yachts – as they still do.

Osborne House became Queen Victoria's favourite dwelling

Freshwater Bay is closely linked with the Victorian poet, Alfred, Lord Tennyson

LITERARY GATHERINGS AT FARRINGFORD

Lord Tennyson, the great poet, leased the Georgian house of Farringford (now a hotel) in 1853 and bought it in 1855 on the proceeds of his poem 'Maud', which he had written there. Tennyson loved to walk on the great green down now named after him, where he said that the air was 'worth sixpence a pint'. The literary lions of the day came to visit: Charles Kingsley, Swinburne, Edward Lear and Charles Dodgson (Lewis Carroll), who is believed to have based the Mouse's Tale in *Alice in Wonderland* on a dream recounted to him by Tennyson himself.

FRESHWATER AND FRESHWATER BAY
Map ref SZ3487/5

The southwest tip of the Isle of Wight which ends in the jagged sea-girt chalk pinnacles of The Needles is known as the Freshwater Peninsula. The village itself is large and bustling, and was made famous by Alfred, Lord Tennyson who came to live at Farringford – now a hotel – in 1853, soon after being proclaimed Poet Laureate. He lived there till 1867 when inquisitive visitors, wishing to see the famous man as he walked on the down in cloak and broad-brimmed hat, drove him to his refuge on the Surrey/Sussex border.

Freshwater has spread south down the western Yar valley towards Freshwater Bay, name of both the little cove and the resort, where, enticed to savour the pleasures of the island by the Tennysons, Julia Cameron, the pioneer portrait photographer, settled in the 1860s. Tennyson sat for her several times, as did other distinguished friends including Charles Darwin and Robert Browning. Eastwards is Alum Bay, with its chair lift and famous cliff of vertical sandstone strata in twelve vibrant colours. The Needles Old Battery is a 19th-century fort with wonderful views, and the Needles Pleasure Park and the modern holiday resort of Totland Bay are popular attractions. The Needles are best viewed via the summer boat trips.

GODSHILL Map ref SZ3281

Nestling prettily beneath its superb 15th-century church tower, this little village of stone-built, thatched cottages is the most visited and photographed place in the whole island. Attractions include the renowned model of Godshill village, the Natural History Centre and the Old Smithy and Gardens. Godshill gets very crowded during the holiday season so try to avoid it when the sun is high – come early in the morning before the coaches arrive or in the evening after they have gone. One peaceful haven is the lovely church, nearly 1,000 years old, which contains a rare medieval wall painting, a painting of Daniel in the lions' den by Rubens (or his school) and monuments to the Worsleys.

Their home, Appuldurcombe House, is now a ruined shell, standing in wooded country to the south amid beautiful grounds landscaped by 'Capability' Brown. Once Hampshire's finest English baroque building, the mansion was built in 1710 for Sir Robert Worsley, whose family had lived at Appuldurcombe for 200 years. A school before the last war, it was bombed so badly in 1943 that it has been uninhabitable ever since. An added attraction here is the Owl and Falconry Centre with its fascinating flying displays.

THE TENNYSON TRAIL

This 13-mile (21-km) trail starts from Carisbrooke and heads southwest up on to Bowcombe Down, then west past many prehistoric tumuli, and into Brighstone Forest, with views over Brighstone Bay. It then heads back up and over onto Mottistone Down and Brook Down before beginning a long descent past the golf course on Afton Down into Freshwater Bay, where it follows the coast path above the cliff. This is Tennyson Down, with a monument to the poet at the high point. The path then drops down into Alum Bay.

Godshill is a honeypot for visitors to the island

**A CYCLE TRAIL FROM
NEWPORT TO YARMOUTH**
The first part of this 18-mile
(28.8-km) tour takes you
alongside the River Medina on
the Newport–Cowes
Cycleway – easy going
because it used to be the
railway line. Follow the river
until West Cowes and
continue round the headland,
past the Castle and Egypt
Point to Gurnard. Beyond
Gurnard, follow the minor
road inland through Rew
Street. Turn left beyond here
and follow the road to Little
Whitehouse, turning left again
to keep the coast on your
right. Continue through
Porchfield and Locksgreen.
Turn right and head down
into Newtown to see the
former village and harbour.

*Newport's arcaded Guild
Hall was designed by John
Nash in 1813*

NEWPORT   Map ref SZ5089

Newport, the capital of the island, is a venerable old
market town on the River Medina. Its squares and
narrow twisting streets may hide the river from the view
of the cursory visitor but boats still ply their trade at the
rejuvenated quay. Here, too, is the arts centre, housed in
a converted warehouse. The pleasant High Street has
many attractive buildings, including the old clock tower
which houses the Museum of Island History, and is
dominated by the Guild Hall with its fine Ionic portico
market by John Nash. St Thomas' Church is the last
resting place of Princess Elizabeth, Charles I's tragic
youngest daughter, who died of a fever at the age of 14
while she was a prisoner in Carisbrooke Castle, just one
month after her father had been sent from here to his
execution.

The town was founded in medieval times as the 'new
port' for the old capital, Carisbrooke, yet, like
Carisbrooke, it can claim to have its roots in Roman
times, since a Roman villa, dating from the 3rd
century AD, was discovered in Avondale Road in 1926.
The villa has been excavated and is open to the public.
Three of the rooms have tessellated floors and the largest
also possesses a fireplace – an unusual feature in a
Roman house. There is also a well-preserved bath suite.

To the northwest of the town is Parkhurst Prison and
beyond it Parkhurst Forest, the remaining glades and
woodlands of a former royal hunting forest. This ancient
woodland, famed for its variety of trees and wild flowers,
is threaded with waymarked paths and is one of the last
refuges for the red squirrel.

NEWTOWN Map ref SZ4290

Newtown was founded in the 13th century by the Bishop of Winchester and its grid-iron pattern can be recognised even today, although only a few houses are left. Its natural harbour was reputed to have anchorage for 50 ships, but continual silting reduced its size and this, coupled with raids by the French, led to the town's decline.

Today the little Town Hall is in the care of the National Trust, and the harbour is a Nature Reserve, echoing to the lonely piping of the curlew and the harsh cry of wild geese passing overhead.

At the head of one of the creeks is Shalfleet, where you can leave your car and explore the old harbour on foot, heading down to the quay which is now busy with pleasure craft. Shalfleet's Church of St Michael was saved in a small-scale replay of the saving of Winchester Cathedral (see page 31). When its stout Norman tower was found to be standing in 10 feet of clay and water and in danger of collapsing, the foundations were relaid in concrete.

The marshes at Newtown are a haven for seabirds

(*continued from previous page*)
Head back up to the coast road, and turn right. When you meet the A road turn right into Shalfleet. Do not take the main road into Yarmouth but strike out down twisting Church Lane and Warlands Lane and at a junction where the old railway used to cross, turn right into Wellow. Continue through Thorley and at the T-junction, turn right past Thorley Manor and the remains of St Swithun's Church and head down to the sea turning left on the A3054 into Yarmouth.

Winkle Street and the Caul Bourne

A pleasant, easy walk along field paths and green lanes close to the tiny Caul Bourne and beneath the wooded slopes of Brighstone Down to the south. One of the most beautiful and unspoilt villages on the island and an historic mill add charm and interest.

Time: 1½ hours. Distance: 3 miles (4.8km).
Location: 5 miles (8km) west of Newport.
Start: Park at Calbourne Mill on the B3401 Newport to Freshwater road.
(OS grid ref: SZ414868.)
OS Maps: Outdoor Leisure 29 (Isle of Wight) 1:25,000.
See Key to Walks on page 121.

ROUTE DIRECTIONS

Walk to the end of the car park, passing **Calbourne Mill**, and take the arrowed path to a stile flanking a gate. Bear diagonally right across a field towards the stream and cross a small brook to a T-junction of paths. Turn left parallel with the brook, through what can be boggy pasture, and shortly pass an old corrugated iron shack, bearing left to two stiles, a footbridge and the B3401.

Cross straight over on to the concrete driveway to Westover Farm. Pass through a gate into the farmyard, follow the track left in front of barns and continue on the stony track along the edge of fields. Descend and pass through Furzebrake Copse, then climb the waymarked stile on the left and follow the path through Withybed Copse to a plank bridge and stile. Keep ahead on defined path across a series of stiles and fields to a stile and footbridge over the Caul Bourne.

Cross the bridge, turn right along the stream edge to a stile, then follow a narrow path to merge with Winkle Street into the picturesque village of **Calbourne.** On reaching a junction, near the entrance to **Westover House**, bear left passing the green and All Saints' Church, then turn left opposite the old village pump into School Lane. Pass beside the Recreation Centre, then keep left along a fence to cross a stile into pasture.

Proceed straight ahead and maintain direction across a series of fields via stiles to reach the B3401 beside Fullingmills Farm. Turn left along the road, cross a bridge, then walk along the right-hand grass verge for a quarter of a mile (0.4km) back to the Mill and car park.

POINTS OF INTEREST

Calbourne Mill

This is one of five mills which once lay along the Caul Bourne to the west of the village. A mill has existed here in this beautiful wooded valley since at least 1299, and the present 17th-century machinery still works when turned by the 20-foot water wheel. It grinds the flour used in producing the home-baked cakes available in the adjacent café. The millpond and stream have been converted into an attractive water garden and the outbuildings house a fascinating display of rural bygones.

Calbourne

Comprising a village green sloping down from an ancient church, a village pump, a white manor house and picture-postcard thatched cottages, Calbourne is one of the most unspoilt villages on

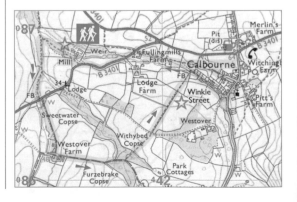

the island. 'Winkle Street' is a delighful piece of old England, with idyllic cottages facing the stream and an old sheepwash – last used in the mid-1970s. All Saints' Church is thought to be the the most complete example of a 13th-century church to be found on the island. It contains a fine brass of William Montacute, son of the Earl of Salisbury, and dates from 1579.

Westover House
The estate dates back to the time of Edward the Confessor. The present fine white-painted Regency house stands in beautiful gardens, and was once owned by Colonel Moulton-Barrett, a relative of Elizabeth Barrett, the poet who married another poet, Robert Browning.

Calbourne Mill, right and idyllic Winkle Street, below

In the days when convicts
were transported to Australia,
most of them left Britain from
ships moored off Ryde – this
town was the last they ever
saw of 'the old country' and
so there remains a special
connection between the two
places. St Thomas' Church,
formerly a ruin, is now a
heritage centre housing an
exhibition commemorating
the sailing of the first ships to
Australia, as well as displays of
local history.

*Hovercraft can bypass the
long pier at Ryde, defying
the shallow water to deposit
passengers straight on to
the shore*

RYDE Map ref SZ5992

Most visitors' first taste of the Isle of Wight is when they
disembark at Ryde from the Portsmouth Ferry. Here,
incongruously, ex-London Transport underground trains
convey them down the half-mile long pier, necessary
because the coast shelves so gently that vessels can get
no closer. It was built in 1813 to end the inconvenience
of a cart ride across the sands from the ferry.

Ryde was developed in the late 18th century and is the
largest town on the island, with some 24,000 residents.
It possesses the usual range of seaside amusements as
well as 5-mile (8-km) long sandy beach. From the
promenade there are superb views across Spithead and
three of the Solent's Victorian forts.

Southwest of Ryde is Brickfields Horse Country,
including the Isle of Wight Shire Horse Centre, while at
Fishbourne, west along the coast, is Quarr Abbey, a
modern foundation (1907–14) of Benedictine monks
near the ruins of the earlier Cistercian Abbey, founded in
1132. The Isle of Wight Steam Railway puffs out of
Smallbrook Junction, just south of Ryde on its journey
past Havenstreet to Wootton.

SANDOWN AND SHANKLIN Map ref SZ5984/5881

The honky-tonk seaside neighbour of more sedate
Shanklin, Sandown was founded as a resort in about
1800 and faces out to sea across Sandown Bay. It is built
at beach level, with the immense chalk walls of Culver
Cliff to the north and the cliffed coast of Shanklin and
Luccombe to the south. Sandown is a popular venue for
family holidays with its sandy beach and an esplanade
and amusement park, a pier of 1878, cinema, the
fascinating Museum of Isle of Wight Geology and
Dinosaur Isle, a museum displaying life-size dinosaurs
and offering guided fossil walks.

Shanklin, the quieter neighbour, is a resort that developed with the coming of the railway in 1891. You reach the beach by lift from the clifftop, which has a superb view around Sandown Bay to the gleaming white heights of Culver Cliff. Inland is Shanklin Old Village, a former fishing village close to the deep winding glen of Shanklin Chine. This 300-feet (91.4-metre) deep wooded and ferny fissure was much beloved of earlier tourists, including the poet, John Keats who stayed at the Old Village in 1819. The Victorians flocked to tread its winding path past the 40-foot (12.2-metre) waterfall to the beach. Today, Shanklin Chine still pulls the crowds – its rare flora is of great interest – and the resort also offers two theatres and a range of seaside amusements.

SEAVIEW Map ref SZ6291

This family holiday resort to the east of Ryde is renowned for its gently sloping, firm sandy beach, from which there is safe bathing. The town still basks in 19th-century charm, with narrow streets lined with villas and shops sloping down to the sea, the peace maintained by the lack of a main through road. Saltern Cottages recall the old salt industry which thrived here on the marshes in the days before Seaview became a select resort for those who shun the bustle and gaiety of Ryde. To the northwest is the famous Flamingo Park, a bird sanctuary on the Slimbridge lines where flamingos, peacocks and waterfowl wander freely over green lawns.

The appeal of Shanklin Old Village has been celebrated for many years

ISLE OF WIGHT RAILWAYS
At one time the Isle of Wight had a comprehensive railway network. Alas, much is gone, but the island's railways are still a haven for transport history buffs. First, there is the surviving British Rail line from Ryde Pier to Shanklin – mostly single track, but electrified and run by veteran ex-London Transport coaches brought over in 1967 and still going strong. At Smallbrook Junction, there's the Isle of Wight Steam Railway which runs for 5 miles (8km) through unspoilt countryside to Wootton, with its headquarters at Havenstreet. It is the perfect complement to the faithful old Ryde–Shanklin electrics, and you can buy through tickets.

THE SOUTHERN CLIFFLINE

The southern coast of the island between Ventnor and St Catherine's Point is a renowned region of massive landslides where great masses of sandstone rock have been, and still are, carried downhill to the sea on a lubricating layer of blue clay, which slips seaward beneath them. Ventnor, in fact, has the biggest urban landslide problem in Britain. The Undercliff, a ledge which extends along the cliffs, is actually the top of an ancient landslide block. In order to appreciate the coast to the full, try part of the coastal path between Shanklin and Blackgang. From Shanklin the path first lies close to, and then on, the shore until Ventnor and beyond. At St Lawrence, the path climbs up beyond the road and affords good views to the south before you reach Blackgang.

The delightful Victorian resort of Ventnor clings to the southern cliffs of the island

VENTNOR Map ref SZ5677

This south coast resort climbs the sheer cliff beneath St Boniface Down, the highest point on the island, as a series of terraces behind the sandy beach, so that the mainly Victorian buildings are stacked in layers and joined by steep zigzagging roads with corkscrew turns. There is something Mediterranean in this arrangement, and Ventnor has been called 'the English Madeira'. The climate, too, is remarkably un-English. Protected from the north by the bulk of St Boniface Down, it basks in sub-tropical conditions.

Prior to 1841, this was a small fishing village – much involved in smuggling – but in that year, a famous doctor, Sir James Clarke, sang its praises and visitors started to come. The railway arrived in 1866 and Ventnor's development as a health resort was assured, attracting, among others, Macaulay, Dickens and Thackeray. Later it was the site of the Royal National Hospital for Consumption and Diseases of the Chest. The town's history is explained in Ventnor's Heritage Museum which includes an extensive archive section.

Ventnor divides into two parts, the elegant 'town' on the cliff-face, where Ventnor ales are still brewed, and the seaside resort at the cliff-foot. The extraordinary climate is manifest in the Ventnor Botanic Gardens where some 3,500 species include palms and cork trees. The Museum of Smuggling History, hidden in subterranean caverns beneath the Botanic Garden, has a large collection of fascinating relics, vividly illustrating the days when Ventnor was the 'headquarters' of illicit trade. Near by is the ancient village of St Lawrence with the Rare Breeds and Waterfowl Park, while Isle of Wight Glass, founded in 1973, produces an exciting range of award-winning glassware.

YARMOUTH Map ref SZ3589

The Lymington–Yarmouth ferry is the picturesque way of entry into the Isle of Wight, for Yarmouth is a compact little town with narrow streets and attractive houses and a small harbour busy with yachts and a flourishing boatbuilders yard (see Walk on page 72). During the Middle Ages it was the most important Isle of Wight town, but decline set in and by 1800 it had only a few hundred inhabitants.

Yarmouth Castle was built against the French in 1547 by Henry VIII and it remained in use until the 1870s. It is hidden down an alley by the ferry, on King's Land, and is missed by many visitors. The pier near the lifeboat station was built in 1876 and was originally the landing stage for the Lymington ferry, but now it is a pleasant walkway from which to view the busy Solent.

West of Yarmouth is Fort Victoria Country Park, based around the remains of a fort built in 1855 to protect the western approach to Portsmouth. The wide grassy areas, coastal slopes, beach and sea wall afford superb views of the Solent, and there are guided walks, a maritime heritage exhibition, a marine aquarium and planetarium.

Historic Yarmouth has a well-hidden castle

A GOVERNOR'S HEAD ON A KING'S SHOULDERS

Yarmouth's church, rebuilt 1614–26, contains an intriguing monument to Sir Robert Holmes, Governor of the Isle of Wight during the reign of Charles II. The figure, supposedly of Sir Robert, was originally intended as a statue of the French 'Sun King', Louis XIV. The statue was being transported by sea so that the sculptor could complete the head from life, but Sir Robert captured the ship carrying it, appropriated the statue and had his own likeness attached instead.

Through the Yar Valley From Yarmouth

A delightful short walk through the Yar Valley incorporating an old railway line and the Freshwater Way. The mudflats of the tidal River Yar are haven to a wealth of waders and ducks – birdwatchers, remember your binoculars! Level and easy going.

Time: 2 hours. Distance: 4 miles (6.4km).
Location: 9 miles (14.5km) west of Newport.
Start: Park in River Road Car Park in Yarmouth.
(OS grid ref: SZ354895.)
OS Map: Outdoor Leisure 29 (Isle of Wight)
1:25,000.
See Key to Walks on page 121.

ROUTE DIRECTIONS

From the car park in **Yarmouth** turn right along River Road and soon turn right again into Mill Road.

Pass the school and Mill Road Garage, then keep ahead on to a track (no through road) beside the **River Yar** and shortly pass the old brick and stone **tidemill**. Follow the riverside path, then bear right on to the disused **Freshwater to Newport Railway** line.

Remain on this picturesque and most peaceful pathway close to the tidal river, pausing from time to time to view the variety of birdlife that congregates on the mudflats. On reaching a minor road, turn right across The Causeway at the head of the estuary and follow the road round into Freshwater village and **All Saints' Church**.

Pass in front of the church and take the path waymarked 'Freshwater Way' beside the Red Lion and proceed alongside the churchyard over two stiles to a track. Cross over on to a rough track and head towards Kings Manor Farm. Just before a barn, turn

The old mill at Yarmouth harbour is a reminder of the town's historic past

left over a double stile and footbridge and follow the arrowed path right along the field edge to the rear of the farm buildings to a stile.

Cross a track and the stile ahead (double gates) and follow the wide track to a gate and junction of paths. Climb the stile on the right, pass through a copse and bear left, uphill, along the field edge. Enter the field on your left and walk along the right-hand edge to a stile. Pass through Saltern Wood to a lane. Bear left to reach the A3054, turn right to cross the Yar swing bridge and right again to return to the car park and the start of the walk.

POINTS OF INTEREST

Yarmouth
Yarmouth is an interesting little town, with stone quays, old houses, a harbour full of boats and a castle that was built by Henry VIII after the French had sacked the town in 1524. It lies tucked away down a passage by the ferry and is in an excellent state of repair, with a hall, parlour, kitchen and open gun platform with splendid harbour views.

River Yar
As well as providing a safe stretch of water for yachtsmen, the River Yar estuary supports a wide variety of wildlife which changes with the seasons. It is a birdwatcher's delight with wintering Brent geese and shelduck swelling the numbers of more common species, such as curlew, oystercatchers, teal, widgeon and herons.
In summer warblers and nightingales can be seen and heard in the reedbanks and copses along the banks of the river.

Tidemill
The tidemill was built in 1793, when the water was deep enough for sailing barges to deliver the corn for grinding. The brick and stone mill has been well restored, and the sluice gates controlling the tidal flow and the old mill pond are still visible.

Freshwater to Newport Railway
Opened in 1889, the Freshwater to Newport Railway offered passengers a particularly pleasant journey along the banks of the River Yar, with tranquil views over marshes and mudflats. Sadly, the line went the way of so many others and closed in 1953.

All Saints' Church, Freshwater
Freshwater was the home of Alfred, Lord Tennyson and his wife Emily from 1853 to their respective deaths in 1892 and 1896. Emily is buried in the churchyard, and various memorials decorate the interior walls. The church stands on a hillock overlooking the River Yar.

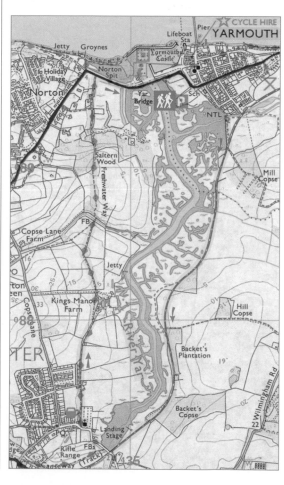

The Isle of Wight

Leisure Information

Places of Interest

Shopping

The Performing Arts

Sports, Activities

and the Outdoors

Annual Events and Customs

✓ Checklist

Leisure Information

TOURIST INFORMATION CENTRES

Cowes
The Arcade, Fountain Quay. Tel: 01983 291914.
Newport
South Street. Tel: 01983 823366.
Ryde
81–83 Union Street. Tel: 01983 562905.
Sandown
8 High Street. Tel: 01983 403886.
Shanklin
67 High Street. Tel: 01983 862942.
Ventnor
High Street.
Tel: 01983 853625.
(Seasonal).
Yarmouth
The Quay. Tel: 01983 760015.

OTHER INFORMATION

English Heritage
Eastgate Court, 195–205 High Street, Guildford, Surrey. Tel: 01483 252000.
www.english-heritage.org.uk
Hampshire and Isle of Wight Wildlife Trust
8 Romsey Road, Eastleigh. Tel: 02380 613636.

Environment Agency
Southern Region, Guildbourne House, Chatsworth Road, Worthing, Sussex. Tel: 01903 832000.
National Trust
35a St James Street, Newport. Tel: 01983 741020.
www.nationaltrust.org.uk

FERRY SERVICES

Car ferries
Portsmouth–Fishbourne (Wightlink) 40 mins.
Southampton–East Cowes (Red Funnel) 60 mins.
Lymington–Yarmouth (Wightlink) 30 mins.
Passenger only
Portsmouth–Ryde (Wightlink) 15 mins.
Southampton–Cowes (Red Funnel) 20 mins.
Southsea–Ryde (Hovertravel) 8 mins.
Hovertravel
Tel: 01983 811000.
Red Funnel
Tel: 02380 334010.
Wightlink
Tel: 0870 582 7744.

ORDNANCE SURVEY MAPS

Landranger 1:50,000. Sheet number 196.
Outdoor Leisure 1:25,000. Sheet number 29 (Isle of Wight).

Places of Interest

There will be an admission charge at the following places unless otherwise stated.
Appuldurcombe House and Owl and Falconry Centre
Wroxall. Tel: 01983 852484. Open mid-Feb to mid-Dec. Flying displays Jun–Sep.
Barton Manor Vineyard and Gardens
East Cowes, on A3021. Tel: 01983 292835. Open Apr to mid-Oct, daily.
Bembridge Windmill
½ mile south of Bembridge on B3395. Tel: 01983 873945. Open late Mar–late Oct, most days.
Brading Roman Villa
Brading. Tel: 01983 406223. Open daily.
Brickfields Horse Country
Newnham Road, Binstead, Ryde. Tel: 01983 566801. Open all year, daily.
Calbourne Water Mill and Rural Museum
Calbourne, on B3401. Tel: 01983 531227. Open Easter–Oct, daily.
Carisbrooke Castle & Isle of Wight Museum
Carisbrooke, on B3401. Tel: 01983 522107. Open all year daily, except 24–26 Dec, 1 Jan.

Cowes Maritime Museum
Beckford Road. Tel: 01983
293341. Open all year, most
days. Free.

Dimbola Lodge
Freshwater Bay. Tel: 01983
756814. Julia Cameron's home,
now restored, with galleries
displaying her contemporary
photographic work. Open most
days.

Dinosaur Farm Museum
Military Road, Brighstone. Tel:
01983 740401. Exhibition of
dinosaur fossils and bones found
along the island's south coast.

Flamingo Park
Springvale, Seaview. Tel: 01983
612153. Open Easter–Oct daily.

Haseley Manor
Arreton. Tel: 01983 865420.
Open Easter–Sep, daily.

Isle of Wight Pearl
Chilton Chine, Military Road,
Brighstone. Tel: 01983 740352.
Open all year, daily.

Isle of Wight Steam Railway
The Railway Station,
Havenstreet. Tel: 01983 884343.
Open Apr–Oct (daily operation
end May–Sep), telephone for
information.

**Lilliput Museum of Antique
Dolls and Toys**
High Street, Brading. Tel: 01983
407231. Open all year, daily.

The Model Village
Godshill. Tel: 01983 840270.
Open Mar–Oct, daily.

Morton Manor Vineyard
Brading, off A3055. Tel: 01983
406168. Open Easter–Oct, most
days.

**Museum of Isle of Wight
Geology**
Sandown Library, High Street,
Sandown. Tel: 01983 404344.
Open all year, most days. Free.

**Museum of Smuggling
History**
Botanic Gardens, The Undercliff
Drive, Ventnor. On A3055. Tel:
01983 853677. Open
Easter–Sep, daily.

The Needles Old Battery
West High Down, Alum Bay.
Tel: 01983 754772. Open end
Mar–late Oct, most days.

Nunwell House & Gardens
Brading. Tel: 01983 407240.
Open end May, then Jul–early
Sep, most days.

Old Town Hall
Newtown, 1 mile (1.6km) north
of A3054. Tel: 01983 741052.
Open late Mar–Oct, limited
opening hours.

Osborne House
1 mile (1.6km) southeast of East
Cowes. Tel: 01983 200022.
Open Apr–Oct, daily.

**Rare Breeds and Waterfowl
Park**
St Lawrence, near Ventnor. Tel:
01983 855144. Open end
Mar–Oct, daily.

Roman Villa
Cypress Road, Newport. Tel:
01983 529720. Open Apr–Oct,
Mon–Sat.

Shanklin Chine
Shanklin. Tel: 01983 866432.
Open early Apr–Oct, daily.

**Shipwreck Centre and
Maritime Museum**
Providence House, Sherborne
Street, Bembridge. Tel: 01983
872223/873125. Open
Mar–Oct, daily.

Sir Max Aitken Museum
High Street, West Cowes. Open
May–Sep, most days.

Tiger & Big Cat Sanctuary
Sandown. Tel: 01983 403883.
Open Easter–Oct, daily.

Ventnor Botanic Gardens
The Undercliff Drive, Ventnor.
Tel: 01983 855397. Open all
year, daily.

Wax Museum
High Street, Brading.
Tel: 01983 407286. Open all
year, daily.

Yafford Mill
Shorwell, nr Newport. Tel:
01983 740610. Open all year,
daily except Jan–early Feb.

Yarmouth Castle
Tel: 01983 760678. Open
Apr–Sep, daily.

SPECIAL INTEREST FOR CHILDREN

**Blackgang Chine Fantasy
Park**
Off the A3055. Tel: 01983
730052. Open Apr–Oct, daily.

The Needles Pleasure Park
signposted on B3322. Alum Bay.
Tel: 01983 752401. Open
Apr–early Nov, daily.

The Model Village
Godshill. Tel: 01983 840270.
Open Mar–Oct, daily.

Shopping

Newport
Open market, town centre, Tue.

Ryde
Open market, Esplanade, Thu.

Sandown
Open market, town centre, Sun
pm.

Ventnor
Market, town centre, Fri
Apr–Christmas.

LOCAL SPECIALITIES

Glass
Alum Bay Glass, Alum Bay. Tel:
08704 580022.
Glory ART Glass, Sandown. Tel:
01983 402515.
Isle of Wight Glass, Old Park, St
Lawrence. Tel: 01983 853526.

Pottery
Chessell Pottery, Chessell, nr
Yarmouth. Tel: 01983 531248.

Wine
Adgestone Vineyard, Brading.
Tel: 01983 402503. Open all
year, Wed–Mon.
Barton Manor Vineyard, East
Cowes. Tel: 01983 292835.
Morton Manor Vineyard,
Brading. Tel: 01983 406168.
Open Easter–Oct, Sun–Fri.
Rosemary Vineyard, Ryde. Tel:
01983 811084.

The Performing Arts

Medina Theatre
Mountbatten Centre, Fairlee
Road, Newport. Tel: 01983
527020.

Quay Arts Centre
Sea Street, Newport. Tel: 01983
528825.
Open daily, times vary.

Shanklin Theatre
Prospects Road. Tel: 01983
868000.

Sports, Activities and the Outdoors

ANGLING

Sea
Excellent sea fishing from the
piers and shores. Contact
Shanklin Tourist Information
Centre for more details.

Fly and Coarse
Island Fish Farm, Brighstone, Tel:
01983 740941.

BEACHES

Alum Bay
Pebble and sand, safe inshore. Chairlift or steps to beach.

Bembridge
Sand and rock pools at low tide, otherwise shingle. Beach huts for hire. Steps to beach.

Bonchurch
Sand and rock pools at low tide.

Brighstone Bay
Sand and shingle.

Brook
Sand. Submerged forest at Hanover Point, fossils in cliffs.

Colwell Bay
Sand at low tide, otherwise shingle. Safe bathing. Dogs not allowed.

Compton Bay
Sand. Steps to beach. Good surfing. Dogs not allowed.

Cowes
East Cowes has Seaside and Solent Water Quality Award. Sand at low tide, otherwise shingle. Dogs not allowed.

Freshwater Bay
Small pebble and shingle beach, sand at low tide.

Ryde
Ryde East has Seaside and Solent Water Quality Award. Sand. Safe bathing. Dogs not allowed.

Sandown
Solent Water Quality Award and Tidy Britain Seaside Resort. Sand. Safe bathing. Fossils in Yaverland and Culver Cliff. Dogs not allowed.

Seaview
Seaside Award and Solent Water Quality Award. Sand at low tide. Safe bathing. Dogs not allowed.

Shanklin
Shanklin North has Southern Water Quality Award and Tidy Britain Seaside Resort Award. Sand. Safe bathing. Steps down to beach. Dogs not allowed.

Totland Bay
Southern Water Quality Award. Sand at low tide, otherwise shingle. Safe bathing. Dogs not allowed.

Ventnor
Sand at low tide. Safe bathing. Dogs not allowed.

Whitecliff Bay
Sand. Steps down to beach. Dogs not allowed.

Yarmouth
Shingle.

BOAT TRIPS

Various boat trips are available around the island.

Cowes Parade, Ryde and Sandown Pier
Solent and Wight Line Cruises. Tel: 01983 564602.

Yarmouth
Contact the local Tourist Information Centre.

COUNTRY PARKS, FORESTS AND NATURE RESERVES

Fort Victoria Country Park, near Yarmouth.
Parkhurst Forest, near Newport.
Newtown Harbour Nature Reserve, Newtown.
Robin Hill Country Park, Downend, Arreton, near Newport. Tel: 01983 730052.

CYCLING

The Isle of Wight is ideal for cycling, with a network of bridleways and attractive minor roads and lanes.

CYCLE HIRE

Cowes
Offshore Sports, 2–4 Birmingham Road. Tel: 01983 290514.

Ryde
Autovogue, 140–140a High Street. Tel: 01983 812989.

Shanklin
Offshore Sports, 19 Orchardley Road. Tel: 01983 866269.

GOLF COURSES

Cowes
Cowes Golf Club, Crossfield Avenue. Tel: 01983 292303.
Osborne Golf Club, Osborne House Estate, East Cowes. Tel: 01983 295421.

Freshwater Bay
Freshwater Bay Golf Club, Afton Down. Tel: 01983 752955.

Newport
Newport Glub Club, St George's Down, Shide. Tel: 01983 525076.

Ryde
Ryde Golf Club, Binstead Road. Tel: 01983 614809.

Sandown
Shanklin and Sandown Golf Club, The Fairway, Lake. Tel: 01983 403217.

Ventnor
Ventnor Golf Club, Steephill Down Road, Upper Ventnor. Tel: 01983 853326.

LONG-DISTANCE FOOTPATHS AND TRAILS

The Isle of Wight Coastal Path
A 60-mile (96-km) trail around the island.

Nunwell House Trail
6½ miles (10.5km) from Ryde to Sandown.

Shepherd's Trail
7½ miles (12km) from Carisbrooke to Atherfield.

Stenbury Trail
9 miles (15km) from Newport to Ventnor.

Tennyson Trail
13 miles (21km) from Carisbrooke to Alum Bay.

SAILING

Cowes
Island Sailing Club, High Street. Tel: 01983 296621.
Royal London Yacht Club, The Parade. Tel: 01983 299727.

Fishbourne
Royal Victoria Yacht Club, 91 Fishbourne Lane. Tel: 01983 882325.

Annual Events and Customs

Cowes
Round the Island Yacht Race; June.
Cowes Week, including Fastnet Race, 1st week in August.
Royal Agricultural Show, late July.

Havenstreet
Steam Extravaganza, August Bank Holiday.

Newchurch
The Isle of Wight Garlic Festival, mid-August.

Ventnor
Crab Fair, May Bank Holiday.

The checklists give details of some of the facilities within the area covered by this guide. Further information can be obtained from Tourist Information Centres.

The Ports and the Southeast Coast

The great Hampshire ports, commercial Southampton and naval Portsmouth, comprise the largest urban area on England's south coast – richly historical, but at the same time at the forefront of modernity. During the 20th century they spread, eating up lesser harbours and towns and creeping inland to wash against the slopes of Ports Down and nudge up the Itchen Valley to Eastleigh. Amongst all this are the

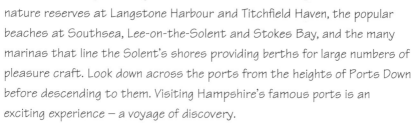

nature reserves at Langstone Harbour and Titchfield Haven, the popular beaches at Southsea, Lee-on-the-Solent and Stokes Bay, and the many marinas that line the Solent's shores providing berths for large numbers of pleasure craft. Look down across the ports from the heights of Ports Down before descending to them. Visiting Hampshire's famous ports is an exciting experience – a voyage of discovery.

BOTLEY Map ref SU5113

William Cobbett, author of *Rural Rides,* lived at Botley between 1804 and 1817 – apart from two years in prison for writing articles criticising flogging in the army. He described this attractive red brick village, where he was constantly quarrelling with the parson, as 'the most delightful village in the world'. Botley remains delightful, its wide main street and busy square dominated by a little porticoed Market Hall of 1848. The mill on the River Hamble, listed in the Domesday Book, still produces flour and animal feeds.

Botley was once a small port at the tidal head of the Hamble – as late as the 1930s timber and corn boats were able to load here. To the south is Manor Farm Country Park, 400 acres of varied habitats supporting a range of plants and animals, with several nature trails. Manor Farm Museum in the country park is a traditional farm largely worked with horses.

WILLIAM COBBETT

Born in 1763, William Cobbett was a self-educated man with forthright views. He fled to America to avoid prosecution, developed his talents as a pamphleteer, but was ruined in a libel suit. Back in England he started his weekly newspaper, *The Political Register*, travelled widely and wrote many books, including *Rural Rides*. In everything he supported the underdog in a pithy and highly opinionated style, adopting radical anti-government views. He was imprisoned for two years, then went back to America, but returned and became a Member of Parliament.

Once a thriving port, Botley has become a peaceful harbour

Emsworth's fortunes have ebbed and flowed over the centuries

POISONED OYSTERS
When the port of Emsworth declined in the 19th century the townsfolk took to dredging for oysters as an occupation. It was one which had to be abandoned with haste when guests at a Winchester banquet died from eating them – they had been polluted with effluent from a new sewer.

EMSWORTH Map ref SU7406
This attractive village was for centuries a thriving port, especially in Georgian times, but that business died out, and the subsequent oyster trade ended in disaster, after which Emsworth became a sleepy, decayed place, with the old oyster smacks rotting where they were left at the head of the marsh-bound harbour. Happily the fortunes of the village revived and it is now a smart yachting centre with a marina.

The old port, sandwiched between two little creeks, is an enchanting tangle of narrow streets and alleys heading down to the water; South Street was once a centre for a smuggling gang, an activity which continued to flourish until Chichester Harbour began to develop more respectably as a sailing centre.

Westwards towards the wilds of Langstone Harbour is Warblington – not a village, but an ancient site, where tall trees and meadows surround the old church, its roof sweeping to the ground, and the ruins of a 16th-century castle. The Solent Way passes this romantic spot.

FAREHAM Map ref SU5606
Fareham's attractive old High Street has a complementary mixture of architecture – 18th-century brick, Victorian stucco and earlier timber. Since World War II the compact old town has expanded and now merges with neighbouring parishes in a sprawl of houses and industry. Nevertheless the centre remains extremely pleasant and visitors can appreciate Thackeray's description of it as a 'dear little old Hampshire town' (he used to spend his school holidays here).

During the Middle Ages Fareham was an important port, until the channels silted up, but prosperity returned in the 18th and 19th centuries with shipbuilding for the Navy, and the big attractive houses on the High Street were built for high-ranking Naval men. Today, there are high-tech industries as well as an entertainment centre and a covered shopping precinct. Fareham Creek, popular with the yachting fraternity, is now a conservation area.

GOSPORT Map ref SU6099

Gosport, across Portsmouth Harbour from the great naval base, is unlovely, but not uninteresting. Reasons to visit include the view across the harbour to Old Portsmouth and the magnificent interior of Holy Trinity Church, containing the organ once played by Handel. The main attraction, though, is the Royal Naval Submarine Museum at HMS *Dolphin*, with many exhibits relating to underwater warfare and submarine development, as well as tours of HMS *Alliance,* a submarine completed at the end of World War II. Gosport's new Millennium Promenade takes in Timespace, one of the world's largest veritcal sundials, and Explosion!, and exciting museum of naval firepower using multimedia, interacative displays and hands-on exhibits.

Gosport's early history is obscure, but it has long been linked with the Portsmouth naval base where its inhabitants worked. In the 1860s, with the fear of a French invasion, Lord Palmerston surrounded Portsmouth with a chain of forts ('Lord Palmerston's Follies') – several on Ports Down and several in Gosport. Fort Brockhurst, in virtually the same state as when it was built, is open to the public.

IRON PUDDLING

In 1784 at Funtley, near Fareham, Henry Cort invented a process of creating wrought iron which helped keep Britain's economy together during the Napoleonic Wars. British iron ores are generally low grade, and during the wars, foreign ores could not get through – a potentially disastrous state of affairs affecting the production of edge tools, agricultural implements, horseshoes and nails. Cort devised the method of 'puddling', whereby the molten metal was stirred with iron bars – a process which separated the ore from the impurities and allowed the production of wrought iron. Little remains today of the iron works, but what there is can be seen beside the footpath off the Wickham–Titchfield road beside the M27.

Fareham's High Street features a charming muddle of architectural styles

The Solent is said to contain the largest pleasure sailing fleet in the world, with over 32,000 yacht berths in the plethora of marinas along the coast from Southampton Water to Chichester Harbour. The sailing is safe here, in the sheltered lagoons of Portsmouth, Langstone and Chichester harbours, in Southampton Water and in the Solent, protected from the open Channel by the Isle of Wight. Hamble is the yachting capital of Southampton Water and Ocean Village, in Southampton's old Alexandra Dock, is a superb marina where hundreds of yachts are moored.

A beautifully kept cottage in North Hayling

HAMBLE   Map ref SU4806

Once the site of flourishing naval dockyards, Hamble and the estuary of the little river which shares its name are very popular with sailors of small pleasure-craft which crowd its waters heading in and out of Southampton Water. The older parts of the village, unpretentious in pleasing brick, wind down to the quayside near the now numerous jetties, the marina and the boatbuilding yards.

Hamble was a favoured place of embarkation during the Napoleonic Wars and troops were mustered here, notably in 1794 when Lord Moira's troops assembled before crossing to Ostend. In more recent times Hamble has had strong links with the aircraft industry, with a British Aerospace factory and airfield where airline pilots were trained. The oil terminal at Hamble Rice on Southampton Water receives oil by pipeline and transfers it to tankers.

HAYLING ISLAND   Map ref SU7202

This low-lying island separates the tidal creeks, mudflats and saltmarshes of Langstone and Chichester harbours. The northern part of the island is chiefly rural while the southern part, facing over the English Channel, has been a resort since the mid-19th century. It has a 5-mile (8-km) long sandy beach, select golf club and all the paraphernalia of a holiday resort devoted to watersports, particularly windsurfing. Drivers should note that there is only one road to and from the island, and it can get very busy.

The seafront is dominated by the huge Norfolk Crescent, erected in the early 19th century, though it was not until the 1930s that the resort really took off. Black Point to the south east and Langstone Harbour to the west are nature reserves and important overwintering grounds for geese and waders. The 13th-century church at South Hayling stands on the island's highest point – the yew tree in the churchyard is a true Saxon, probably 1,000 years old; the Saxon font is one of only a handful of that age in Hampshire.

NETLEY ABBEY   Map ref SU4508

Netley, a Victorian town on the shores of the Solent, was formerly important for three things – its castle, its abbey and its gigantic military hospital, the Royal Victoria, built in the aftermath of the Crimean War. It was demolished in 1966 and the site is now occupied by the pleasant Royal Victoria Country Park. It covers over 100 acres of woods, marshes and beach, and includes a nature trail and various walks.

The ruins of Netley Abbey stand thoughtfully brooding in woodland next to the Solent shore. It was founded in 1239 as a daughter house of Beaulieu and, as little is known of goings on here, we must assume a peaceful and prayerful existence on the part of the monks, till the dissolution 300 years later. Netley Castle, on the shore close to the Abbey, was one of Henry VIII's coastal gun stations – its tall tower is Victorian, and it has been transformed into a wonderful folly with all the panoply of Gothic device.

BIRDWATCHING AT LANGSTONE HARBOUR
Langstone Harbour is the central of the three shallow lagoons of the south coast and, while Portsmouth Harbour and, to an increasing extent, Chichester Harbour, are developed, Langstone remains for the most part a wild, saltmarsh-girt, muddy place. The harbour itself covers some 5,000 acres and contains a 1,370-acre RSPB reserve, at its best in September and through the winter when it is full of migrant waders, sometimes as many as 20,000 of them, including Brent geese, dunlin, turnstones and rare black-tailed godwits. There are frequent sightings of resident oystercatchers, redshanks, herons and shelducks.

The royal chapel, now a museum, is all that remains of the great military hospital at Netley

Within the strong walls of Portchester Castle lies a chapel, the remnant of a 12th-century Augustinian priory

THE SAXON SHORE

The Roman fort was one of the chain of defences built on the North Sea and Channel coasts in late Roman times against the marauding Saxon pirates, and for this reason they were known as the Forts of the Saxon Shore. It was probably the *Portus Adurni* mentioned in the late Roman document the *Notita Dignitatum*, and is associated with Carausius, Roman 'Count of the Saxon Shore', who turned rebel and ruled Britain independently for ten years until he was murdered.

PORTCHESTER CASTLE Map ref SU6105

This is one of the most fascinating historical sites in Britain. The massive, 20-foot (6-metre) high walls of a 3rd-century Roman fort sit on a little promontory on the northern shore of Portsmouth harbour, facing directly across it and out to sea. These noble walls, 10 feet (3 metres) thick, enclose a rectangular area of 9 acres – the most complete Roman fort in northern Europe.

After the Roman withdrawal from Britain, Portchester's defences were left much as they were until 1133 when a priory was founded here by Henry I. Within ten years it had moved inland to Southwick, but Portchester's parish church is a survivor of the monastic foundation. In 1153 the Normans took over the abandoned fort and built a keep on the northwest corner, plus a wall and moat enclosing an inner bailey. The castle was further fortified at regular intervals throughout history and in 1415 Henry V mustered his troops on the greensward of the outer bailey and led them through the Water Gate to embark for France and the Battle of Agincourt.

Subsequently it was used as a Royal country house and in 1535 Henry VIII and Anne Boleyn stayed here and were 'very merry' – a year later Anne went to the scaffold. Did their daughter Elizabeth I think of this when she stayed at Portchester in 1601, an old lady on her last 'progress' through her realm?

PORTSMOUTH Map ref SU6400

Portsmouth has been Britain's foremost naval base since the late 15th century, when it had the first ever dry dock, and is now just as famous for its historic ships which can be visited in the Naval Dockyard. HMS *Victory*, launched in 1765, was Nelson's flagship at the Battle of Trafalgar in 1805 and is probably the most famous of all British warships; she is the oldest commissioned warship in the world. The *Mary Rose*, pride of Henry VIII's fleet, was launched at Portsmouth in 1511, rebuilt to carry more guns in 1536 and sank off Southsea in July 1545, sailing to meet the French in battle, and in full view of the king who was watching from Southsea Castle. The remains of her wreck were raised in 1982 and are now housed in a specially constructed building. 'Permanent conservation' is under way, and there is an exhibition of the of artefacts found during the salvage. HMS *Warrior*, the first 'ironclad', was launched at Blackwall in 1860, the largest, fastest and most formidable warship the world had ever seen. The Dockyard also houses the redeveloped Royal Naval Museum and Action Stations, a thrilling high-tech Royal Naval experience using film and interactive technology.

BOAT TRIPS AROUND THE HARBOUR

Try to take one of the boat trips around Portsmouth Harbour – with their running commentaries, they give a genuine taste of seafaring Portsmouth: modern naval vessels, ferries and the general hustle and bustle of this most important of naval ports. At the very least catch the little ferry over to Gosport, for a view back to Old Portsmouth, it is a delightful picture.

The view of Old Portsmouth from Gosport

Nelson's glorious flagship,
Victory, *is among the*
historic ships on display in
Portsmouth harbour

A GRANDSTAND VIEW

Ports Down is a long ridge of
chalk with spectacular views
across Portsmouth and
Southampton Water. At night
it is a great sea of lights; by
day, a pair of binoculars make
all the difference to the fun of
ship-spotting. At the western
end of the down is the tall
stone obelisk to Lord Nelson.
Survivors of the fleet each
subscribed two days' pay
towards its construction. Ports
Down is also known for
'Palmerston's Follies', massive
brick forts of the 1860s built
during the height of fears of a
French raid. What is surprising
is that attack was expected
not from the sea, but by land
from the north.

During World War II Portsmouth was bombed very
heavily and it is unfortunate that much of the rebuilding
has been particularly uninspired – one building was
voted the ugliest in Britain by readers of a Sunday
newspaper. This being so, hurry through to the historic
dockyard and then follow the Millennium Promenade
(Renaissance Trail) on foot through the bustling
Gunwharf Quays complex to The Point. This is the
oldest and most picturesque quarter of Old Portsmouth,
where attractive old streets survive and have been
restored, and faces out onto a little harbour called
Camber. This area of intricate little roads and attractive
Georgian and Victorian houses was known as 'Spice
Island', an invocation of the exotic cargoes that arrived
here. Walk on the old defences or linger by the seawall
in Bath Square to watch the world and the shipping go
by – this is the best of Portsmouth.

The city has 12 museums, including Charles Dickens'
Birthplace in Old Commercial Road, but the City
Museum and Art Gallery in Museum Road is probably
the best place to start. It features 'The Story of
Portsmouth' and will point you in the direction of the
remaining historic buildings around the city, including
the Landport Gate of 1760, the Square Tower of 1494
and the Royal Garrison Church, where Catherine of
Braganza (who had arrived at Portsmouth under naval
escort six days earlier) married Charles II in 1662.

SOUTHAMPTON   Map ref SU4112

Modern Southampton has been made by its docks, and its docks have made modern Southampton. Its famous double tides give prolonged high water, and although the main docks are not accessible to the public, there's a grand view of the comings and goings of the big ships and the pleasure craft from Western Esplanade and Town Quay.

This is a large, exciting city and port, with its huge Civic Centre, the first ever built, its university, famed for its scientific approach, and the Hall of Aviation, which offers hands-on experience of many of the exhibits (try your hand at a supersonic jet!). Here too is the R J Mitchell Museum, a memorial to the designer of the renowned Spitfire fighter plane which was built at Southampton's Supermarine Works. A Spitfire is included among the exhibits.

Southampton is not all modernity – it is an ancient place with a wealth of antiquities in its historic core. There was a Roman harbour, *Clausentium,* on the eastern bank of the River Itchen at modern-day Bitterne, but Southampton itself began life as 'Hamtun', a Saxon settlement important enough by the 8th century to have Hampshire named after it.

Southampton grew rapidly under Norman rule as the port between Normandy and the English capital at Winchester. Bugle Street, the best-preserved old street in Southampton, was part of the Norman town. By 1300 Southampton was one of England's most important ports, and its history can be traced in the Maritime Museum, housed in an enormous medieval warehouse beside Town Quay.

TRANSATLANTIC SEAPORT

Southampton's passenger liners plied the Atlantic Ocean from late Victorian times until the 1960s, reaching their heyday in the 1920s and '30s. These voyages to New York have taken on a legendary air. Before the days of air travel, everyone who needed to cross the ocean had to do so by sea, and Southampton was the stylish equivalent of Heathrow. Entertainers, artists, socialites – all travelled through the huge Terminus Station at Southampton to embark at Ocean Dock and later at the New Docks along the River Test, large enough for eight of the world's largest liners to dock at the same time. After World War II the transatlantic trade blossomed into an Indian Summer, with the famous Queens, *Queen Mary* and *Queen Elizabeth,* carrying on a weekly service.

Southampton is still the home port of some of the world's great ocean liners

Southampton's medieval walls are a surprise survival

THE OLD WALLS OF SOUTHAMPTON

Southampton's image is of so much modernity that it seems incredible that it should possess some of the best-preserved medieval town walls in England. They were built all the way round the town in the 12th century, a protection against French raiders, who elsewhere frequently burnt down coastal towns. Immediately west of Bugle Street a great deal survives, including the West Gate. Footbridges and walkways aid access. Magnificently strong, the walls and their associated buildings are, in all Southampton, the one thing not to be missed.

The historic entrance to the town is along the A33 from Winchester, passing the huge, gloriously shaggy common which has existed in much the same shape since the 13th century, and continuing along The Avenue and into Southampton at Bargate, the impressive northern gateway.

Southampton was decimated by World War II bombing, but the magnificent medieval Church of St Michael miraculously survived. Many of the elegant 18th- and early 19th-century houses that succeeded the timber ones have gone, but the Dolphin Hotel, where Jane Austen attended the winter assemblies when she lived in nearby Castle Square, stands to this day, calmly surveying the world from its huge semi-circular bay windows.

High Street leads down to the waterside at the old Town Quay, now a shopping and office complex and gloriously maritime as it juts out into the harbour. Near by on Western Esplanade is the site of the vanished West Quay, with its memorial to the Pilgrim Fathers. This was the point from which they originally sailed in two ships in 1620, thinking never to set foot on English soil again. They were forced to put into Plymouth and there abandon the leaking *Speedwell,* to continue crowded together in *Mayflower.*

The most spectacular of Southampton's antiquities, and the most astonishing wartime survival is the great length of the 12th-century town walls to the west of Bugle Street.

SOUTHSEA Map ref SU6599

Beyond the tangle of Old Portsmouth's streets to the east, you emerge on to Southsea Common, faced by imposing terraces of 19th-century stucco. The splendid grassy common overlooking the sea escaped development in the 19th century because it was used for military training, and we must be eternally grateful for this as it gives Southsea its distinctive flavour. Southsea developed as a residential suburb of Portsmouth, but the seaside location transformed it into a holiday place from the 1860s onwards.

Today there is a raucous funfair near the hovercraft terminal for the Isle of Wight at Clarence Pier. The wide Clarence Esplanade, between the common and the sea, has the big Naval War Memorial, an aquarium and the interesting Southsea Castle Museum. The D-Day Museum near by contains the remarkable Overlord Embroidery, a tapestry of the events of June 1944.

Further east the pier provides boat trips and amusements while on East Parade is the Natural History Museum. The Royal Marines Museum is housed in Eastney Barracks, beyond which are the Port Solent and Eastney Marinas. The Solent Way passes along the whole of Southsea front.

OFFSHORE FORTS

During the 1860s four sea forts were built offshore, part of the great ring of forts designed to protect Portsmouth and Spithead from a feared attack by the French. The smallest is Spit Bank Fort, which had provision for nine 38-ton guns and can be visited by ferry from Southsea pier – a most unusual tourist attraction!

Southsea Castle guards the entrance to Portsmouth harbour

The Wriothesley monument in Titchfield church

THE SOLENT WAY

This 60-mile (96-km) path runs from Milford on Sea via Southampton and Portsmouth to the wild saltings of Langstone Harbour and Emsworth. The stretch from Warsash (or Hamble) to Emsworth begins along an undeveloped stretch of Solent coast between the Hamble River and Titchfield Haven, at the mouth of the River Meon, where there is a nature reserve. Beyond Titchfield Haven it goes past the beach at Lee-on-the-Solent and the lovely curve of Stokes Bay, turning inland at Gilkicker Point for the ferry from Gosport to Old Portsmouth. From here it passes Southsea to the edge of Langstone Harbour, before curving round to Emsworth.

TITCHFIELD Map ref SU5405

Titchfield, situated on the lower reaches of the River Meon is an attractive village of twisting roads with a delightful High Street. On the outskirts are modern aerospace factories – creating a curious juxtaposition of ancient and modern. In medieval times Titchfield was a market centre for the surrounding area and a prosperous port, with a large and thriving Abbey, founded in 1232 and now in the care of English Heritage. At the Dissolution the abbey passed to Thomas Wriothesley, the 1st Earl of Southampton, who converted part of it into a house, but it fell into disrepair in the 18th century and is now in ruins. Very little of the original abbey remains, but the plan has been established on the ground. A 15th-century tithe barn stands near by.

The 1st Earl also instituted a land reclamation scheme, damming the mouth of the river and building a canal (now in the nature reserve of Titchfield Haven). One of England's earliest canals, it was too small for merchant ships and Titchfield's days as a port were over. The Earl has not been forgiven, and his effigy is burnt at the 5th November celebrations organised by the Bonfire Boys.

A different – and magnificent – effigy of the Earl is to be found in the south chapel of the church. The famous Wriothesley Monument by Gerard Johnson, a Flemish refugee, was carved in 1594 and shows the 1st Earl with his wife and son. The 3rd Earl was a friend of Shakespeare and it is said that some of his plays received their first performance here.

The Ports and the Southeast Coast

Leisure Information
Places of Interest
Shopping
The Performing Arts
Sports, Activities and
the Outdoors
Annual Events and Customs

Checklist

Leisure Information

TOURIST INFORMATION CENTRES

Fareham
Westbury Manor, West Street.
Tel: 01329 221342.
Gosport
Museum, Walpole Road. Tel:
02392 522944.
Hayling Island
Seafront, South Hayling.
Tel: 02392 467111.
(Seasonal).
Portsmouth
The Hard.
Tel: 02392 826722.
Southampton
Above Bar Precinct. Tel: 02380
221106.
Southsea
Clarence Esplanade. Tel: 02392
826722.

OTHER INFORMATION

Countryside Commission
John Dower House, Crescent
Place, Cheltenham, Gloucester.
Tel: 01242 521381.
English Heritage
Eastgate Court, 195–205 High
Street, Guildford, Surrey. Tel:
01483 252000.
www.english-heritage.org.uk

**Hampshire and Isle of
Wight Wildlife Trust**
8 Romsey Road, Eastleigh. Tel:
02380 613636.
Environment Agency
Southern Region, Guildbourne
House, Chatsworth Road,
Worthing, Sussex. Tel: 01903
832000.
National Trust
Southern Region, Polesden
Lacey, Dorking, Surrey. Tel:
01372 453401.
www.nationaltrust.org.uk
RSPB
South East Regional Office, 2nd
Floor, 42 Frederic Place,
Brighton, West Sussex.
Tel: 01273 763600.

ORDNANCE SURVEY MAPS

Landranger 1:50,000. Sheet
numbers: 196, 197.

Places of Interest

There will be an admission
charge at the following places of
interest unless otherwise stated.
**Charles Dickens Birthplace
Museum**
393 Old Commercial Road,
Portsmouth. Tel: 02392 827261.
Open Apr–Sep, daily; first 3
weeks Dec and 7 Feb.

**City Museum, Art Gallery &
Records Office**
Museum Road, Portsmouth.
Tel: 02392 827261. Open all
year, daily, except Public Hols &
Christmas.
**D-Day Museum and
Overlord Embroidery**
Clarence Esplanade, Southsea.
Tel: 02392 827261. Open all
year, daily, except Christmas.
Eastleigh Museum
25 High Street. Tel: 02380
643026. Open all year, most
days. Free.
Explosion!
Priddy's Hard, Gosport. Tel:
02392 505600. Open daily.
Fareham Museum
Westbury Manor, West Street.
Tel: 01329 824895. Open all
year, most days. Free.
Fort Brockhurst
Gunner's Way, Elson, Gosport.
Tel: 02392 581059. Open all
year, daily in summer.
God's House Tower
Winkle Street, Southampton.
Tel: 02380 635904. Open all
year, most days except Bank
Hols.
Gosport Museum
Walpole Road. Tel: 02392
588035. Open all year, most
days. Free.

Manor Farm Museum
Pylands Lane, Bursledon. Tel:
01489 787055. Open
Easter–Oct, daily; Nov–Easter,
Sun only.
The *Mary Rose* Museum
Her Majesty's Naval Base,
Portsmouth. Tel: 02392 861512.
Open daily, closed 25 Dec.
Medieval Merchant's House
58 French Street, Southampton.
Tel: 02380 221503. Open
Apr–Oct, daily.
**Natural History Museum
and Butterfly House**
Cumberland House, Eastern
Parade, Portsmouth. Tel: 02392
827261. Open all year, daily,
except Christmas.
Netley Abbey
Tel: 01732 778000. Open Etr–
Oct; wknds out of season. Free.
Portchester Castle
Off A27. Tel: 02392 378291.
Open all year, most days.
Portsmouth Aquarium
Clarence Esplanade, Southsea.
Tel: 02392 875222. Open daily.
Royal Marines Museum
Eastney Barracks, Portsmouth.
Tel: 02392 819385. Open all
year, daily, except 24–26 Dec.
Royal Naval Museum
Her Majesty's Naval Base,
Portsmouth. Tel: 02392 861512.

Open daily.
**Royal Naval Submarine
Museum and HMS *Alliance***
Haslar, Jetty Road, Gosport. Tel:
02392 529217. Open all year,
most days, closed 24 Dec–1 Jan.
**Southampton City Art
Gallery**
North Guild. Civic Centre. Tel:
02380 832277. Open all year,
most days. Free.
**Southampton Maritime
Museum**
The Wool House, Town Quay.
Tel: 02380 223941. Open all
year, except Mon. Free.
Southsea Castle Museum
Clarence Esplanade. Tel: 02392
827261. Open Apr–Sep, daily.
Titchfield Abbey
Tel: 02380 226235. Open daily.
Free.
Tudor House Museum
St Michael's Square,
Southampton. Tel: 02380
332513. Open all year, most
days. Free.
HMS *Victory*
Her Majesty's Naval Base,
Portsmouth. Tel: 02392 861512.
Open daily.
HMS *Warrior*
Her Majesty's Naval Base,
Portsmouth. Tel: 02392 861512.
Open daily.

The following places of interest
may be of interest to visitors
with children. Unless otherwise
stated there will be an
admission charge.
Manor Farm Museum
Pylands Lane, Bursledon. Tel:
01489 787055. Open
Easter–Oct, daily. Nov–Easter,
Sun only.
Portsmouth Aquarium
Clarence Esplanade, Southsea.
Tel: 01705 734461. Open 14
Apr–Dec, daily, except 25 Dec.

Shopping

Eastleigh
Market in town centre, Thu and
Sat.
Fareham
Market in town centre, Mon.
Main shopping area, Fareham
Shopping Centre.
Gosport
Market in town centre, Tue and
Sat.
Portsmouth
Market in town centre, Thu, Fri
and Sat.

The formidable bulk of HMS
Warrior, *Portsmouth*

Main shopping area,
Commercial Road Precinct,
Cascades, Gunwharf Quays.
Southampton
Market in town centre, Thu, Fri
and Sat.
The main shopping areas are:
Bargate Shopping Centre, East
Street, Marlands Shopping
Centre, Ocean Village, West
Quay.

The Performing Arts

Guildhall
Civic Centre, Southampton. Tel:
02380 632601.
King's Theatre
Albert Road, Southsea. Tel:
02392 828282.
Mayflower Theatre
Commercial Road,
Southampton. Tel: 02380
711811.
New Theatre Royal
20–24 Guildhall Walk,
Portsmouth. Tel: 02392 649000.
Nuffield Theatre
University Road, Southampton.
Tel: 02380 671771.
The Portsmouth Arts Centre
Reginald Road, Southsea. Tel:
02392 837373/732236.

Sports, Activities and the Outdoors

ANGLING

Sea
Gosport: Fishing from Stokes
Bay.
Southampton: Free fishing from
public footpath between
Woodmill and Mansbridge.
Fishing on Southampton Water
for pout, whiting and eels.
Southsea: Fishing from Southsea
Pier

BEACHES

Gosport
Stokes Bay. Sand and shingle.
Safe bathing.
Hayling Island
Sand. Safe bathing.
Lee-on-the-Solent
Shingle beach. Safe bathing.
Netley
Shingle, with mud at low tide.
Southsea
Shingle. Safe bathing except at
eastern end and harbour mouth.

BOAT TRIPS

Hamble
Boats for hire and boat trips
from Hamble.
Portsmouth Harbour
Various boat trips around the
harbour: Blue Boats, tel: 02392
822584.
Gosport Ferry Company, tel:
02392 524551.
Portsmouth Harbour Boat Trips,
tel: 02392 839766.
Portsmouth Harbour Tours, tel:
02392 739459.
Southampton
Various boat trips available with
Blue Funnel Cruises, Ocean
Village, Southampton. Tel:
02380 223278.

CRICKET

Southampton
County Cricket is played at the
Southampton Common ground.
Tel: 02380 333788.

COUNTRY PARKS, FORESTS AND NATURE RESERVES

Black Point Nature Reserve,
Hayling Island.
Itchen Valley Country Park,
Eastleigh. Tel: 02380 466091.
Langstone Harbour.
Royal Victoria Country Park,
Netley. Tel: 02380 455157.
Titchfield Haven. Tickets from
Haven House Visitor Centre, Cliff
Road, Hill Head, Fareham. Tel:
01329 662145.
Manor Farm and Country Park,
Botley. Tel: 01489 787055.

FOOTBALL

Portsmouth
Portsmouth Football Club,
Fratton Park, Frogmore Road.
Tel: 02392 731204.
Southampton
Southampton Football Club, The
Friends Provedence, St Mary's
Stadium, Britannia Road. Tel:
0870 220 0000.

GOLF COURSES

Botley
Botley Park Hotel, Golf and
Country Club, Boorley Green,
Botley. Tel: 01489 780888.
Eastleigh
Fleming Park Golf Course,
Passfield Avenue. Tel: 02380
612797.

Fareham
Cams Hall Estate Golf Club,
Cams Hill. Tel: 01329 827222.
Hayling Island
Hayling Golf Club, Links Lane.
Tel: 02392 464446.
Lee-on-the-Solent
Lee-on-Solent Golf Club, Brune
Lane. Tel: 02392 551170.
Portsmouth
Great Salterns Public Course,
Burrfields Road. Tel: 02392
664549.
Rowlands Castle
Rowlands Castle Golf Club, Links
Lane. Tel: 02392 412784.
Shedfield
Marriot Meon Valley Hotel &
Country Club, Sandy Lane. Tel:
01329 833455.
Southampton
Chilworth, Main Road,
Chilworth,. Tel: 02380 740544.
Southampton, Golf Course
Road, Bassett. Tel: 02380
760478.
Southsea
Southsea, The Clubhouse,
Burrfields Road. Tel: 02392
664549.
Stoneham
Stoneham Golf Club, Monks
Wood Close, Bassett. Tel: 02380
769272.

LONG-DISTANCE FOOTPATHS

The Solent Way
60-mile (96-km) path running
from Milford on Sea to
Emsworth.

Annual Events and Customs

Netley
Hampshire County Show. Royal
Victoria Country Park, weekend
in August/September.
Portsmouth
Navy Days, alternate years.
Trafalgar Day Ceremonies, HMS
Victory, late October
Southampton
International Boat Show, mid-
September.
Titchfield
Carnival. Dates vary from year to
year – check with local Tourist
Information Centre.

The Eastern Hill Country

A great swathe of hill country stretches across eastern Hampshire – first the westerly extension of the South Downs, with the South Downs Way along their crest, then the downs break into a series of ridges rising to Old Winchester Hill, Beacon Hill and Butser Hill, all with superb views.

Through this gentle chalkland scenery runs the River Meon, in its glorious valley with lovely villages. North of the lively old town of Petersfield, the hill country changes dramatically. Nicknamed 'the Alps', its sharp ridges, clothed with hanging beech woods, alternate with intricate little valleys, diminutive streams and little lost villages. It is an intense, inward-looking landscape, full of surprises, where it is impossible to travel quickly.

BOLES' LAST STAND

During the Civil War, Alton's church saw the desperate last stand of the Royalist Colonel John Boles, who, with a band of 80 men, was trapped in Alton by a large contingent of Parliamentarians. They fought through the streets from one house to the next before barricading themselves into the church. Finally overwhelmed, they were massacred, and bullet marks are still visible on the great oak south door. A brass recalls the colonel's death in the pulpit, surrounded by a ring of dead Parliamentarian soldiers whom he had slain.

Oliver Cromwell stayed at this house in Church Street, Alton

ALTON   Map ref SU7139

This is an attractive town, known for its brewing industry, but in earlier times Alton was famous for cloth manufacture, with bombazine and barragon among the fabrics made – names redolent of another age!

The double-naved Church of St Lawrence is mostly 15th century but retains its central Norman tower with 11th-century carvings of dragons, birds and beasts. A large, rather florid cross in the churchyard marks the grave of eight-year-old Fanny Adams, brutally murdered in 1867. Frederick Baker was hanged for the crime, but the phrase 'Sweet Fanny Adams' passed into the English language, deriving from the black humour of naval ratings of the time, who were being served tinned meat.

Alton's Curtis Museum, founded in memory of the 18th-century botanist, William Curtis, has good natural history and geology sections, and displays on local history and archaeology, while the Allen Gallery in Church Street has an excellent collection of pottery and porcelain. The Mid Hants Railway, 'the Watercress Line', connects here with the main line after its 10-mile (16km) journey from Alresford (see page 13).

BISHOP'S WALTHAM   Map ref SU5517

This bustling little place lays claim to be one of Hampshire's most attractive small towns and was planned and laid out in the 13th century. Its streets, with the exception of High Street, are very narrow and hurry towards the focal point of the town, George Square, with its pleasant 17th- and 18th-century buildings. Bishop's Waltham, as the name suggests, was the seat of the Bishops of Winchester, who first acquired it in AD 904, and only parted with it as recently as 1869.

In 1136 Bishop Henry de Blois, brother of King Stephen, built the palace which now stands in ruins on the west side of the town. Over the next few centuries the palace was enlarged, probably by the great bishop, William of Wykeham, who died there in 1404, and certainly by Bishop Langton in 1493–1501. During the Civil War, in 1644, it was captured by Parliament, after the bishop had fortified himself inside with 200 Royalist soldiers. The bishop managed to escape in a dung cart, and Cromwell's men proceeded to reduce the buildings to their present condition, albeit one of Hampshire's most impressive ruins.

Substantial remains of the ruined bishops' palace, Bishop's Waltham

BREWING IN ALTON

Alton has been a celebrated brewing town since the 17th century, and once several breweries faced each other across the High Street. Today, only the Bass Brewery remains at Manor Park, where a brewery guide takes you step by step through the brewing process. At the end of the tour you may sample the brew, a habit of travellers through the ages, as shown by an incident in Thackeray's *Vanity Fair*. In the novel, Joseph Sedley returned to England from India in the year 1817. He landed at Southampton and drove to London – it was the pre-railway era. 'At Alton', Thackeray wrote, 'he stepped out of the carriage at his servant's request, and imbibed some of the ale for which the place is famous'.

IRON-AGE FARM PROJECT

This working reconstruction shows how Iron-Age farmers lived some 2,300 years ago. The animals kept are the nearest modern equivalents to prehistoric breeds, including Soay sheep, Dexter cattle and Exmoor ponies, and the crops grown include primitive varieties of wheat, spelt and emer. The fenced compound is effectively an Iron-Age farmyard with goat pen, hayrick and the main farm building – the round house.

The reconstructed Iron-Age farm below Butser Hill

BUTSER HILL   Map ref SU7120

At 810 feet (247 metres), the highest point on the South Downs, Butser Hill is a superb viewpoint from which, on a clear day, you will see for 40 miles (64.4km) to the spire of Salisbury Cathedral. It is a great whale-backed grassy down, cut by deep, steep coombes, the summit partly enclosed by Iron-Age earthworks that probably define a hilltop pasture rather than a fort. It is still grazed by a flock of sheep and in summer there are sheep husbandry demonstrations. There is a convenient car park close to the summit, but it's a tremendous hill to climb, and the huge view deserves to be the reward for some effort. Below the hill, on the eastern side of the A3 in Chalton Lane, is Butser Ancient Farm, a reconstruction of an Iron-Age farm of about 300 BC, centred on a thatched round house which is 36 feet (11 metres) high, with a diameter of 42 feet (12.8 metres). Its walls are made of woven oak stakes with hazel rods, daubed with clay, and inside is a replica oven and open hearth. The walls are hung with goat and sheep hides, tanning in the smoke of the domestic fires. Other working replicas include a pottery kiln, an upright loom for weaving wool and a hand mill for grinding flour.

Butser Hill is part of the 1,400-acre Queen Elizabeth Country Park, with abundant wildlife as well as plenty of waymarked trails, picnic sites and a Forest Centre. The many leisure pursuits available include pony trekking and orienteering, hang-gliding and grass skiing.

CHAWTON Map ref SU7037

This is Jane Austen's village – a pretty little place with thatched cottages, just to the south of Alton, and now bypassed by the main road which used to pass close to Jane Austen's house. The famous novelist came to Chawton in 1809 with her mother and sisters to live at a house renovated by her brother, Edward, who had just inherited Chawton House. Here she wrote some of her best loved works: *Mansfield Park*, *Emma* and *Persuasion*.

The unpretentious brick house that Jane loved so dearly is now a museum dedicated to her memory. It contains many of her and her family's possessions, including much of the original furniture, and the rooms have been restored as she would have known them. Also preserved is the little donkey carriage in which she travelled around the village when she was too ill to walk. Jane Austen died in 1817 shortly after moving to Winchester, and is buried in the great cathedral. Her mother and sister Cassandra are buried in the churchyard at Chawton. There is also a book shop and a delightful flower-filled garden.

Legend has it that former inhabitants of Clinkers Forge in the village used to keep evil spirits at bay by preserving a mummified cat and rat in the roof. To the southwest is Chawton Park Woods, run by the Forestry Commission, with waymarked paths through the coniferous plantations.

The Austens referred to their Chawton home as 'the cottage'

LITERARY HAMPSHIRE

The variety of landscape of the eastern hill country seems to hold a particular attraction for the muses – Edward Thomas, the writer and poet killed in World War I, lived for a time at Steep, north of Petersfield (see Walk on page 100). Just over the hills is Selborne, the lifelong home of naturalist Gilbert White (1720–93). His great work, *The Natural History and Antiquities of Selborne*, is an enchanting collection of letters, the fruits of 40 years of the application of a keen mind to the ways of the wildlife in his own corner of Hampshire. Further north is Chawton, where Jane Austen lived from 1809–17.

ILLEGAL CRICKET

Cricket was once made illegal because people were betting large sums of money on matches; the penalty for playing was a £10 fine and two years' imprisonment. In 1748, however, cricket was legalised, described as 'a legal and very manly game, not bad in itself, but only in the ill use made of it by betting more than ten pounds on it'. The Hambledon Cricket Club was founded in 1750, but the sport still attracted gambling, and rather like horse racing today, it became a game that attracted people from both extremes of the social scale, all of them keen to bet wherever they could. Thus it was that for the big matches, such as Hambledon v All England, the players were hand-picked and the matches played for heavy stakes, usually £500 a side.

East Meon was well established by the time of the Domesday Book

HAMBLEDON Map ref SU6414

Hambledon means cricket, or at least the history of cricket. The Hambledon Club was founded in 1750 and in 1774 laid down the rules of the game as played today. The club played on a fine natural ground two miles (3.2km) away up on Broadhalfpenny Down. Here, the noble granite monument and the Bat and Ball pub, full of cricket memorabilia, keep alive the heyday of the club, when the Hambledon eleven repeatedly trounced a team drawn from all England.

The village, down in the wooded valley, is a pleasant place with red brick Georgian houses and one or two much photographed timber ones. High Street is the focal point and leads to the Church of Saint Peter and Saint Paul – a strange mixture of styles: the nave hints at Saxon work, there was a Norman enlargement, it was added to throughout the Middle Ages and finally restored by the Victorians. In the churchyard lie the mortal remains of several famous cricketers.

MEON VALLEY

The valley of the River Meon is one of the most beautiful in Hampshire, with a sparkling chalk stream flowing past attractive villages, through meadows and woodlands (see Car Tour on page 102). The river rises near East Meon, regarded as Hampshire's loveliest village with a superb Norman church which is visible for miles around. The river babbles along its High Street before meandering to West Meon, still pleasant despite the thunderous traffic. Thomas Lord, the founder of Lord's Cricket Ground in London, is buried in the churchyard.

At Warnford, where watercress beds are prominent, the Norman church escaped restoration in the 1890s because the autocratic Lord of the Manor refused to let anyone touch it. At the time he was considered misguided; today we can be thankful. It stands in stunningly beautiful parkland, which also contains the mysterious ruin of a 13th-century building, commonly known as King John's House, though its associations are with the St John family.

Below Warnford the valley is deeper and more sheltered and the little stream passes four villages: delightful Exton, has a wide grassy space bordering the swiftly flowing water; Corhampton has an extraordinary 9th-century church, with a sundial on the south wall, divided not into 24 hours but into 8 'tides', the Saxon method of counting time that vanished for ever under Norman rule; idyllic Meonstoke shows its best face to the river, not the road; Droxford was a favourite with Izaak Walton, who came to fish and to stay with his daughter, who had married the rector. Droxford was the secret location where Churchill and Eisenhower, aboard a train in the railway sidings, endured a 24-hour wait and then gave the order for the D-Day invasion. Today a 9-mile (14.4-km) stretch of the trackbed makes a superb walk from West Meon to Wickham.

The next village below Droxford is straggling Soberton, beyond which the valley becomes wider and shallower, passing from the chalk rocks on to clay and sands and so it arrives at Wickham (see page 105). Below this pleasant old town, the wide, shallow river flows into the Solent at Titchfield Haven.

IN PRAISE OF THE VALLEY
The natural beauty of the Meon Valley has been extolled over the years, even by William Cobbett, not known for uttering words of praise. Over a century later the great topography writer, H J Massingham, vowed that he would rather spend his last days in the Meon Valley than anywhere else in England. The virtues of the river itself have also been sung, notably by Izaak Walton, that prince of fishermen, and by many others since his time.

THE MEONWARA
Legend holds that this deep, verdant valley kept the Meonwara – the men of Meon – isolated for centuries from the outside world, and maintains that you may, even today, find here the tall, dark and intelligent Jutish types.

The church at Warnford was founded by Wilfrid of York

Old Winchester Hill is a famous vantage point

THE SOUTH DOWNS WAY

The South Downs Way is the most famous long-distance path in Southern England. It is easy to see why, for this exhilarating walk runs for the most part on the top of the downs, affording spectacular views; to the north over the Weald and to the south over the coast. The walk is over 100 miles (161km) long, from Winchester in the west and heading east along the downs' crest as they slowly converge on the sea, ending in the spectacular cliffs of Beachy Head. It passes through the heart of this region, the highlight being the ascent of Butser Hill, the highest point on the downs and a superb viewpoint. You can take a detour to lovely East Meon, and then head back up to splendid Old Winchester Hill, crowned by an Iron-Age hillfort.

OLD WINCHESTER HILL   Map ref SU6220

This is a splendid hilltop above the River Meon, with views far across Hampshire and the Isle of Wight. It is not known how the hill came by its name, since it is 10 miles (16km) from Winchester as the crow flies. It is crowned by an oval-shaped hillfort enclosed by a single bank and ditch, with the rampart still standing to a height of 18 feet (5.5 metres). It has not been excavated but probably dates from the 2nd century BC. A group of barrows lies to the west of the fort.

The hill is now a National Nature Reserve with beech woodlands, clumps of juniper – rare in Hampshire – belts of big yews and plenty of scrub and thorn, which collectively harbour a varied wildlife. The chalk grassland is very rich in wildflowers. Some people claim that there are ghosts here, that at times the place has a strangely charged atmosphere. And why not? A long history, a superb site and magnificent views: the world would be a poorer place if such a combination did not make something stir in the shadows.

PETERSFIELD   Map ref SU7423

An attractive country town lying in a wide valley, Petersfield retains an atmosphere at once genteel and active. The fine old square in the town centre, now pleasantly pedestrianised, is watched over by the once-gilded figure of William III, in Roman dress and mounted on a charger. The square possesses some good Georgian buildings and there is plenty of architecture of merit around the town. The well-known Petersfield Bookshop attracts lovers of second-hand books from all over the country. (See Car Tour on page 102.)

Street names speak of Petersfield's past as an important market for the wool trade: Sheep Street, which leads off Market Square, and The Spain, which was the haunt of Spanish wool merchants. On a different note, Music Hill is where the military bands played in the 18th century.

During the coaching era Petersfield was an important staging post on the London–Portsmouth road, with as many as 27 coaches passing through daily, bringing brisk trade to the inns. There were a large number competing for the custom, especially the important Navy personnel and dignitaries.

The delightful walled Physic Garden, just off the square, is planted with herbs renowned through the ages for their medicinal properties. It was given to the Hampshire Gardens Trust in 1988 by Major John Bowen. Another horticultural connection is that Petersfield was home to John Goodyer, the pioneer botanist, who was born in Alton in 1592. He lived at a time when plants from the New World were first being cultivated among the useful herbs of English country gardens and he observed and recorded vast numbers of plants in the gardens, lanes and fields around the town. He recorded the first English potatoes and named many plants familiar to us today. Goodyer worked some 40 years before the 'father of botany', Linnaeus, and a century before Gilbert White. To the southeast of the town is Petersfield Heath, with an attractive lake, known as Heath Pond, and about 20 round barrows.

CYCLE EAST HAMPSHIRE'S BYWAYS

This 15-mile (24-km) ride explores the hilly unspoilt country to the north west of Liss. Head through West Liss, turn left on a minor road to Hawkley, then go southwest out of Hawkley following the minor road past Prior's Dean Church. Continue and bear left, then over a crossroads and carry on until a road joins from the right. Just beyond, turn right to the White Horse, a rare survival of a country pub. Return to the fork in the road and turn left for East Tilstead. Take the minor road to Selborne, 3 miles (4.8km) distant, then return to Liss.

An equestrian statue of William III commands Petersfield's main square

In the Steps of Edward Thomas

An undulating ramble among the beech hangers of 'Little Switzerland', affording stunning views towards the South Downs, and across farmland around the village of Steep. This beautiful part of East Hampshire was much loved by the Edwardian poet Edward Thomas. Some tracks can be very muddy.

Time: 3 hours. Distance: 4½ miles (7.2km).
Location: 2 miles (3.2km) north of Petersfield.
Start: From the centre of Petersfield head west on the A272, crossing the railway. At the roundabout take 2nd exit, signposted 'Steep'. Go through Steep, up the hairpin hill and at the top turn right into Cockshott Lane (unmetalled) where there is a small parking area. (OS grid ref: SU734268.)
OS Map: Explorer 133 (Haslemere & Petersfield) 1:25,000.
See Key to Walks on page 121.

ROUTE DIRECTIONS

From the parking area walk back along Cockshott Lane, passing **Red House** on your left, then just before the junction, take the arrowed path left and descend steeply down Ashford Hill into Lutcombe Bottom.

At the lane turn left, passing **Berryfield Cottage** and Ashford Chace on the right.

Cross the waymarked stile on the right to a track beside Ashford Chace. In 300 yards (274 metres) bear left to a stile into woodland. Keep to this path, parallel with the Ashford Stream and lakes, then just past the Conservation Viewing Point, bear right downhill over a footbridge to a lane near a waterfall and the the Old Mill.

Turn right, then take the arrowed path left into pasture, opposite a junction of lanes. Proceed ahead, keep close to the woodland to cross a plank bridge and stile into woodland. Follow the stony path, soon leave the trees and cross a playing field to a lane opposite **All Saints' Church** in Steep. Turn left, then at a sharp right-hand bend, bear left with waymarker into woodland. Keep right immediately and descend to a stile on the woodland fringe.

Head towards the left-hand field corner, cross two stiles and follow the path around

The view of the South Downs from Shoulder of Mutton Hill was a favourite

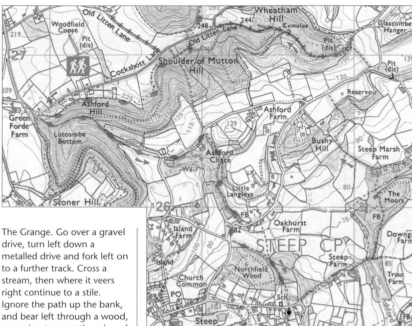

The Grange. Go over a gravel drive, turn left down a metalled drive and fork left on to a further track. Cross a stream, then where it veers right continue to a stile. Ignore the path up the bank, and bear left through a wood, emerging to cross the edge of a garden to an isolated cottage. Cross the drive, proceed through woodland, pass to the left of large sheds, then bear left at fingerpost to cross a footbridge and stile.

Keep along the right-hand edge of the field and continue beside woodland before bearing right across a stile. Bear half-left across pasture, following waymarkers, cross a stile and ascend a narrow footpath to a lane. Turn right, then in a quarter of a mile (0.4km), just after a junction, cross the arrowed stile on the left, and take the avenue of trees uphill to a stile on the woodland edge. Turn left on to Old Litten Lane and climb steeply up Wheatham Hill through beech woods. Along the summit, keep to the main track, diverting left a short distance along the **Hangers Way** to **Shoulder of Mutton Hill** and the memorial to Edward Thomas. Return to the track, following it back to the car park.

POINTS OF INTEREST

Red House
Edward Thomas and his family lived in the area from 1906 to his untimely death during World War I in 1917. They lived for four years in the Red House, high up among the beech hangers above Steep, and his poems 'The New House' and 'Wind and Mist' were inspired by the house.

Berryfield Cottage
Berryfield Cottage was the poet's first home in the area, and it was from here that he first explored the beech woods and mysterious coombes of the Hangars which inspired his work. Most of his writing refers to the years that he resided in Steep.

All Saints' Church, Steep
The part-Norman church contains two small lancet windows which were designed and engraved by Laurence Whistler. They were installed in 1978 on the centenary of Edward Thomas's birth. While you are here, take time to look at the charming kneelers, which depict rural scenes.

Hangers Way
This 21-mile (33.6-km) linear path runs south from Alton Railway Station to Petersfield through some of the most beautiful and varied scenery in the county.

Shoulder of Mutton Hill
A sarsen stone erected here in 1937 is dedicated to Edward Thomas's life and work. It was a favourite spot of his, from which magnificent views unfold 'sixty miles of South Downs at one glance', as Thomas described it.

Hill Country of Selborne and the Meon Valley

Starting in the pleasant town of Petersfield, this 60-mile (96.6km) tour plunges immediately into an intricate landscape of secluded valleys and wooded hills. It loops through Selborne, home of the naturalist, Gilbert White, and out into the enchanting Meon Valley, before passing over high downland past Hambledon and Butser Hill.

ROUTE DIRECTIONS

See Key to Car Tours on page 120.

Leave Petersfield heading northwest towards Steep. Bear right at the roundabout on to the unclassified road signed 'Alresford, Froxfield, Steep'. Cross the bridge over the A3 to Steep. Turn right at the crossroads by The Cricketers pub and then left into Mill Lane. Continue along the winding lane for about 1¼ miles (2km) and then take the left-hand fork (not Steep Marsh). In a quarter of a mile (0.4km) turn right signed 'Liss, Hawkley', carry on to the T-junction and turn left signed 'Hawkley'. Go up the steep zigzag hill. Hawkley village lies to your left. Turn right at the telephone box, signed 'Empshott, Selborne', and bear left with the lane going downhill and across a stream. Bear right through Empshott and turn left on to the B3006 into Selborne.

In Selborne turn left opposite the church into Gracious Street. At the T-junction in about 1¾ miles (2.8km) turn left into Newton Valence. Continue over the staggered crossroads, signed 'Hawkley'. Turn right, signed 'Priors Dean, Colemore'. Go over the hill and bear right where the lane forks. Keep on to a T-junction, turn left, go straight over the crossroads and continue ahead for 1¾ miles (2.8km).

Bear left opposite Bower Farm and in half a mile (0.8km) turn right at the T-junction, signed 'Froxfield Green, East Meon'. Continue, going over a crossroads, to the A272 Petersfield–Winchester road. Cross the A272 on to the unclassified road opposite. In 1½ miles (2.4km) turn right at the T-junction into East Meon.

Turn left into the village, turn right and then left into Chapel Street. Continue past Duncombe Farm and Coombe Cross, turn left and then right at Coombe. Turn right at the next crossroads and continue with Old Winchester Hill, site of an Iron-Age camp, on your left. Continue, bearing left, to reach the A32 on the edge of Warnford and turn left, then take the second right turn, signed 'Winchester 10'. Continue for 1½ miles (2.4km), turn left at the crossroads, then left again, passing around the crown of Beacon Hill. Go straight on, signed 'Unsuitable for wide vehicles'.

Follow the road down into the Meon Valley at Exton. Turn right over the River Meon and cross the A32 on to the unclassified road. Immediately turn right, heading through Corhampton. At the T-junction, bear right into Meonstoke, then fork left for Droxford.

Continue ahead, turn left

Looking down to Selborne from the Hanger

on to the B2150, signed 'Waterlooville, Hambledon', passing under the Meon Valley railway bridge. Immediately turn right, signed 'Soberton'. Continue to Soberton, turn right at the crossroads beyond the village, follow the road round into High Street and fork right at the war memorial, signed 'Swanmore'. Continue ahead and turn left on to the A32 to Wickham.

Turn left on to the B2177, signed 'Southwick' for 2½ miles (4km). Take the third left turn, signed 'Denmead' and continue for 3½ miles (5.6km) to join the B2150. Bear left into Hambledon.

Bear right in Hambledon where an unclassified road forks from the B2150, signed

'Clanfield, Petersfield', and continue to the **Cricket Ground Monument** and The Bat and Ball pub on Broadhalfpenny Down. Go straight on and into Clanfield. Turn left, and then bear right. Turn immediately left into North Lane and follow it towards Butser Hill (superb view on left). At the junction turn right (detour straight on to the Butser Hill picnic site).

Turn left, signed 'Petersfield, Portsmouth', then turn right, signed 'Portsmouth', on to an unclassified road. Turn left at the roundabout, taking the bridge over the A3. The windmill to the right crowns the aptly named Windmill Hill. Turn left, passing **Butser Ancient Farm**, a reconstructed Iron-

Age farmstead. Follow the road to Chalton. Turn left before the church, signed 'Ditcham, Idsworth, Compton', and go over the hill. Turn left and follow the winding road bordering the **Queen Elizabeth Country Park**. Go under the railway to Buriton. Turn right at the crossroads, continue past the church (North Lane) and on for 1½ miles (2.4km) to turn left on to the B2146. Pass Heath Pond on your right and continue into Petersfield.

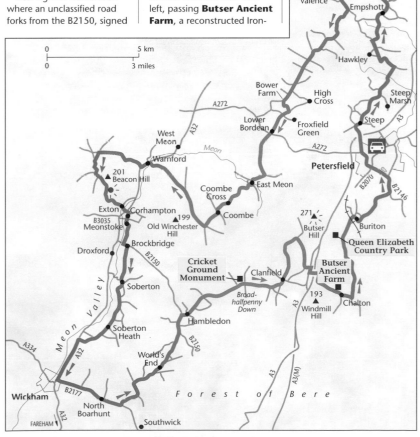

THREE REMARKABLE MEN

At The Wakes at Selborne the honours are shared by three remarkable men, Gilbert White, Francis Oates and Captain Lawrence Oates, uncle and nephew, who were explorers. Francis travelled widely, bringing back tales of tropical wonder, while his nephew was destined to perish on Scott's ill-fated expedition to the South Pole in 1912. Captain Oates was one of those who actually reached the Pole. During the struggle back he suffered from severe frostbite and, fearing that he was slowing down the party, he walked out into a heavy snowstorm and was never seen again. Shortly before he too perished, Captain Scott wrote in his diary that the action of Captain Oates was 'the act of a very gallant gentleman'.

Selborne remains a characterful little village

SELBORNE   Map ref SU7433

Tucked in its little valley amid a maze of intricate lanes beneath the great hanging woods of beech, Selborne used to be known for its great Augustinian priory, founded in 1233. Today it is renowned as the former home of Gilbert White, the naturalist curate, whose enchanting *Natural History and Antiquities of Selborne*, published in 1788, has become a classic. This little book has elevated White to the top ranks of natural history pioneers.

Gilbert White was born in Selborne in 1720, died there in 1793 aged 72, and is buried in the churchyard. He was particularly fond of Selborne Hanger, the steep, beech-clad hillside above the village crowned by a stone called The Wishing Stone, and of the wide common above, from which there are magnificent views. The zigzag path up which he climbed still exists and both the hanger and the common are protected by the National Trust, as is much of the attractive village.

Gilbert White's home, The Wakes, is now the Gilbert White Museum. It also houses the Oates Museum, commemorating both the explorer Francis Oates and his nephew Captain Lawrence Oates who perished with Scott in the Antarctic. Selborne wears its fame lightly, and is a busy, friendly place, centred on a handsome green called The Plestor which lies opposite The Wakes, and there are attractive houses and cottages. The Church of St Mary dates from about 1180 and has impressive Norman arcades, and White's fine memorial window depicting St Francis of Assisi preaching to 82 birds.

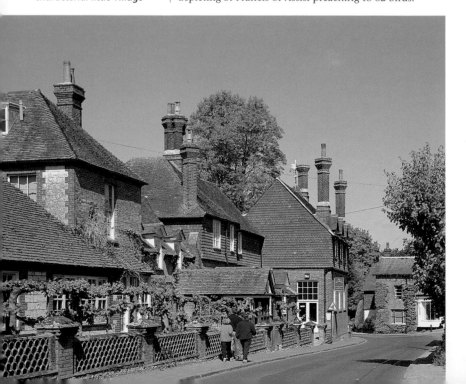

Above, kneeling figures on the memorial to William Uvedale

Left, flint-knapped and retaining traces of its Norman origins in the main doorway, Wickham's church stands alone at the eastern end of the village

WICKHAM   Map ref SU5711

William of Wykeham, the famous Bishop of Winchester and Chancellor of England, was born in this market town in 1324, and something of the grandeur of the great man's reputation seems still to hang over his birthplace. The central square, the very best in Hampshire, would be very fine indeed, with its mellow red brick houses, many of them sporting shops, were it not for the modern housing at one end and the use of the open space mainly for car parking. Yet, why complain? Wickham is a real and vibrant place.

Wickham is a Meon Valley settlement and owes its existence to the river, many of its former industries harnessing water power, including the former tannery and brewery. One mill, Chesapeake Mill, was rebuilt in 1820 using timbers from the American frigate *Chesapeake,* captured in a famous naval battle in 1813 by HMS *Shannon.* The Church of St Nicholas, of Norman date but much restored by the Victorians, stands aloof from the town on a roundabout. It was severed from the rest of Wickham when the Meon Valley Railway was built in 1905.

WICKHAM FAIR

Wickham still holds its annual fair, granted by charter of Henry III in 1268 – and held every year since then, even during the war. Today it may be mostly a funfair, but even this holds to a long frolicsome tradition. Moreover, the custom still lingers of taking a pony to a pub to give it a pint!

The Eastern Hill Country

✓ **Checklist**

Leisure Information

Places of Interest

Shopping

Sports, Activities and
the Outdoors

Annual Events and Customs

Leisure Information

TOURIST INFORMATION CENTRES

Alton
7 Cross and Pillory Lane. Tel:
01420 88448.
Petersfield
County Library, 27 The Square.
Tel: 01730 268829.

OTHER INFORMATION

Countryside Commission
John Dower House, Crescent
Place, Cheltenham, Gloucester.
Tel: 01242 521381.
English Heritage
Eastgate Court, 195–205 High
Street, Guildford, Surrey. Tel:
01483 252000.
www.english-heritage.org.uk
**Hampshire and Isle of
Wight Wildlife Trust**
8 Romsey Road, Eastleigh. Tel:
02380 613636.
Environment Agency
Southern Region, Guildbourne
House, Chatsworth Road,
Worthing, Sussex. Tel: 01903
832000.
National Trust
Southern Region, Polesden
Lacey, Dorking,
Surrey.
Tel: 01372 453401.
www.nationaltrust.org.uk

RSPB
South East Regional Office, 2nd
Floor, 42 Frederic Place,
Brighton, West Sussex. Tel:
01273 763600.

ORDNANCE SURVEY MAPS

Landranger 1:50,000. Sheet
numbers 185, 186, 197

Places of Interest

There will be an admission
charge at the following places of
interest unless otherwise stated.
Bear Museum
38 Dragon Street, Petersfield.
Tel: 01730 265108. Open all
year, most days. Free.
Bishop's Palace
Bishop's Waltham. Tel: 01489
892460. Open Apr–Oct, daily.
Bohunt Manor Gardens
Petersfield Road, Liphook. Tel:
01429 722208. Open all year,
daily.
Butser Ancient Farm
Butser Hill, near Petersfield. Tel:
02392 598838. Open Apr–Oct,
daily.
**Curtis Museum and Allen
Gallery**
Alton. Tel: 01420 82802. Open
all year, most days. Free.
**Gilbert White's House and
The Oates Museum**
The Wakes, High Street,

Selborne. Tel: 01420 511275.
Open Jan–24 Dec, daily.
**Hollycombe Steam
Collection**
1½ miles (2.4km) southeast of
Liphook, on unclassified road.
Tel: 01428 724900. Open Apr to
mid-Oct, Sun & BH; 22 Jul–27
Aug, daily.
Jane Austen's House
Chawton, Alton. Tel: 01420
83262. Open Apr–Oct, daily,
certain days rest of year.
**Mid Hants Railway (The
Watercress Line)**
The Railway Station, Alton. Tel:
Alresford Station 01962 733810.
Open May–Sep, most days;
weekends Feb–Oct.
Physic Garden
rear of 16 High Street,
Petersfield. Tel: 01730 264457.
Open all year, daily.

SPECIAL INTEREST FOR CHILDREN

The following places of interest
may be of interest to visitors
with children. Unless otherwise
stated there will be an admission
charge.
**Hollycombe Steam
Collection**
1½ miles (2.4km) southeast of
Liphook, on unclassified road.
Tel: 01428 724900. Open Apr to
mid-Oct, Sun & BH; 22 Jul–27

Aug, daily.
Mid Hants Railway (The Watercress Line)
The Railway Station, Alton. Tel: Alresford Station 01962 733810. Open May–Sep, most days; weekends Feb–Oct.

Shopping

Alton
Open-air market, town centre, Tue.
Petersfield
Open-air market, town centre, Wed and Sat.

LOCAL SPECIALITIES
Craft workshops
The Old Granary Art and Craft Centre, Bank Street, Bishop's Waltham. Tel: 01489 894595.
Wine
Meon Valley Vineyard, Hill Grove, Swanmore. Tel: 01489 890180. Open Easter–Sep.

Looking over the Queen Elizabeth Country Park from the viewpoint of Butser Hill

Wickham Vineyard, Botley Road, Shedfield. Tel: 01329 834042. Open daily.

Sports, Activities and the Outdoors

COUNTRY PARKS, FORESTS AND NATURE RESERVES
Alice Holt Forest Visitor Centre Bucks Horn Oak, near Farnham. Tel: 01420 23666. Open Apr–Sep, daily.
Chawton Park Woods, near Chawton.
Old Winchester Hill, near East Meon.
Petersfield Heath, just south of Petersfield.
Queen Elizabeth Country Park, near Petersfield. Tel: 02392 595040. Open Apr–Oct, daily.
Steep Marsh Nature Reserve, just north of Petersfield, near Steep.
Wealden Edge Hangers, north of Petersfield.

GLIDING
Lasham
Lasham Gliding Society, Lasham Airfield. Tel: 01256 384900.

GOLF COURSES
Alton
Alton Golf Club, Old Odiham Road. Tel: 01420 82042.
Bordon
Blackmoor Golf Club, Bordon. Tel: 01420 472775.
Liphook
Old Thorns Hotel, Golf and Country Club, Griggs Green, Liphook. Tel: 01428 724555.
Liphook Golf Club, Wheatsheaf Enclosure. Tel: 01428 723271.
Petersfield
Petersfield Golf Club, Heath Road, Petersfield. Tel: 01730 262386.

LONG-DISTANCE FOOTPATH
South Downs Way.
Over 100 miles (161km) long, from Winchester to Beachy Head.

Annual Events and Customs

Petersfield
Hampshire Country Fair, Queen Elizabeth Country Park. Early July.

The Northeast Heathland

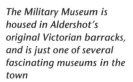

Northeastern Hampshire is gently undulating, generally low-lying, with chalk hills rising to the south and west. Here on the clay plain, in stark contrast, are the charming small town of Odiham and big, busy Basingstoke. To the east the land rises to the sandy heaths, wild stony tracts of scrub and pines with birches and gorse, dominated by the military towns of Aldershot and Farnborough. Northeast Hampshire is rich in great houses: The Vyne, a superb Tudor building and the Duke of Wellington's great house at Stratfield Saye. Hidden among the leafy lanes near the Berkshire border is one of Britain's most intriguing archaeological sites, the decaying walls that enclosed the important Roman town of Calleva at Silchester.

THE HEROES SHRINE

In Aldershot's Manor Park is the Heroes Shrine, the national memorial to the dead of World War II, which consists of rockeries made with stones from bomb-damaged buildings.

ALDERSHOT Map ref SU8650

The British Army town above all others, Aldershot was a little village on open heathland even as late as 1850. Recognising the value of the wild heaths for military training, the government bought 10,000 acres and built the first permanent military camp in Britain since the Roman occupation. Aldershot is the largest of Britain's military camps and its museums provide an interesting insight not only into the history of this famous camp, but also of airborne forces (including Germany and the United States), of army transport, of physical training, of army nursing and dentistry (soldiers once had to bite through paper cartridges when loading muskets, so strong teeth were essential).

The Military Museum is housed in Aldershot's original Victorian barracks, and is just one of several fascinating museums in the town

BASINGSTOKE   Map ref SU6352

Basingstoke, which was mentioned in the Domesday Book, was once a sleepy old market town which burst into life once a week when the cattle market was held in the town square. During and for 15 years after World War II the town began to develop as an industrial centre for modern engineering and pharmaceuticals, but its essential character, that of a country town, remained unchanged. Now the old town is swamped by the huge expansion which began in the 1960s, with dual carriageways, office blocks and pedestrian precincts, developed as part of the London overspill plan.

Some of old Basingstoke still exists, to be sought out and admired: the pleasant old main street, the ruined 13th-century Chapel of the Holy Ghost and its neighbour the 16th-century Holy Trinity Chapel, also ruined, romantically set in a corner of the cemetery. The Old Town Hall, built in 1832, now houses the Willis Museum, which includes a collection of clocks, and the Haymarket of 1864 is now a theatre. Church Cottage, a lovely Elizabethan building stands beside the restored 14th-century Church of St Michael the Archangel.

Modern Basingstoke has much to offer including The Anvil, a major concert hall, a large pedestrianised shopping centre and an extensive leisure park where you will find Milestones. Here 19th- and early 20th-century street scenes bring Hampshire's recent history alive with the transport, sounds and smells of the times.

Old almshouses of painted brick, Basingstoke

MILESTONES – HAMPSHIRE'S EXCITING LIVING HISTORY MUSEUM
At Milestones in Basingstoke visitors can wander down cobbled streets, chat to staff in period costume, discover shops and factories of days gone by along with the collections of Hampshire's industrial and everyday life. Agricultural and commercial vehicles are on display along with an AA motorbike and sidecar and other yellow vehicles which form part of the AA Collection.

Hartley Wintney is an antiques-hunter's paradise

NAPOLEON'S TOMB

Farnborough has an unusual claim to fame, for here lies the end of the Napoleonic dream. In an extraordinary mausoleum of 1877, in the true French Flamboyant style, lie the mortal remains of the Emperor Napoleon III, his son the Prince Imperial and his wife the Empress Eugenie. Farnborough seems a strange and unlikely place for the final act of the heroic Napoleonic saga, but the Empress Eugenie came to live at Farnborough Hill, a large house which she made even larger, after the death in exile of her husband and then of her son. Adjacent to the mausoleum is St Michael's Abbey, also built by the Empress as a memorial. She lived on at Farnborough till her death, visiting her native Spain at the age of 95 in 1920.

FARNBOROUGH Map ref SU8753

Farnborough and Aldershot merge imperceptibly, both military towns that were small heathland villages until the 1850s. Farnborough, though, has airborne associations, which began when the military ballooning base was moved to the town from Woolwich. His Majesty's Ballooning Factory grew into the Royal Aircraft Factory and then the Royal Aircraft Establishment, which is still at Farnborough and names among its many functions the investigation of air disasters.

It was at Farnborough in 1908 that Samuel Cody, from Texas, made the first powered flight in Britain. He flew at Laffan's Plain, an area long since submerged in the development of Farnborough Airfield where these days the famous international air show is held biennially, attracting some quarter of a million visitors from all corners of the globe.

HARTLEY WINTNEY Map ref SU7656

Hartley Wintney's glory is its common and the great green spaces that separate the clumps of housing, for this village, once an important coaching stage, has no outstanding architecture, though it has won awards for upkeep and appearance. Tradition maintains that cricket has been played on the green since 1770 – a pleasant thought – while the row of oaks on the common, known as the Mildmay Oaks, were planted after the Battle of Trafalgar by the lady of the manor to provide timber for future ships. They are unlikely to be needed by the modern navy, and long may they continue to form the present fine spectacle, adding to the beauty of these green spaces.

St Mary's churchyard holds the bones of Field Marshall Alanbrooke, of World War II fame, and, notoriously, General Henry Hawley who earned the nickname 'Hangman' during the 1745 Jacobite Rebellion. He lived at nearby West Green House, a charming and peaceful oasis with a walled garden, herbaceous borders and flowering shrubs. Three miles (4.8km) north of Hartley Wintney is Eversley, where the author Charles Kingsley was vicar from 1844 to 1875. The wrought iron school gates are a memorial to him.

ODIHAM Map ref SU7451

Unselfconscious Odiham has survived the 20th century as a genuine small market town, and certainly possesses some of Hampshire's best townscapes. The High Street is every bit as good as the better-known New Alresford and Fareham, lined by houses with elegant Georgian façades, many of them tacked on to older buildings, with plenty of architectural detail to delight the enthusiast.

Narrow streets lead off from the High Street, and the big 14th-century church with its distinctive 17th-century brick tower stands among them to the south. A large open space – The Bury – to the north of the church still has stocks and a whipping post and near by is the tiny 17th-century Pest House, the place of confinement for residents who caught the plague. It now houses a small private museum.

To the north are the ruins of Odiham Castle. King John rode forth from here in 1215 on his way to meet the barons at Runnymede where he was forced to sign the Magna Carta. All that remains of the castle today is an octagonal keep, one of only two of that shape in England.

THE BASINGSTOKE CANAL
The Basingstoke Canal has had a chequered history. It opened in 1794, linking the River Wey at Weybridge with Basingstoke – a distance of 37 miles (59.5km) – but traffic was always light and it struggled to pay its debts. There were grand plans to make it a through route, but the arrival of the London–Southampton railway in 1846 dealt the fatal blow. The canal lingered on, in and out of trouble, until 1914, when traffic between Woking and Basingstoke ceased; the collapse of Greywell tunnel near Odiham closed this section in 1932, but boats continued to Woking until 1949. Greywell tunnel, now home to a large colony of bats, and the M3 prevent a complete reopening, but much of the canal has now been restored and there are boat trips from Odiham.

A 14th-century king of Scotland was imprisoned in Odiham Castle

The grass-covered ruins of Basing House

CAUGHT IN THE SIEGE

One of the more surprising facts about the siege of Basing House is that both the famous architect, Inigo Jones, and the engraver Wenceslas Holler, were among the survivors taken into captivity.

Moreover, a tradition states that Cromwell's raiders attacked at so unlikely a moment that they disturbed the defenders playing cards, which has led to the old Hampshire saying 'Clubs are trumps, as when Basing House was taken'.

OLD BASING Map ref SU6854

Two miles (3.2km) east of Basingstoke, and in a different world, is Old Basing, once the more important settlement. It is a pleasant place with narrow streets and many old thatched cottages. On its outskirts are the celebrated ruins of Basing House, once the largest private house in Tudor England, built within the ramparts of a medieval castle. The house was ransacked and thrown down in the Civil War after holding out against a Parliamentary army for over two years, one of the longest sieges England has ever witnessed.

The siege began in 1643 when the house was defended by the Royalist Marquess of Winchester and a force of 500 men. As the two years dragged by, with bouts of heavy fighting and intervals so quiet that supplies could get through, all the non-Catholics deserted and others died of disease. At length, in October 1645, Cromwell himself arrived, flushed with his success in taking Winchester, and his storming parties broke through the defences early one morning.

SILCHESTER Map ref SU6261

This is one of the most extraordinary Roman sites in Britain, a walled Roman town which was deserted after the Roman occupation and never again inhabited save that a Norman parish church was built within the walls near the former east gate. Silchester was *Calleva Atrebatum*, 'the town in the woods belonging to the Atrebates', the British tribe who founded it shortly before the Romans arrived, and who rebuilt it on Roman lines in AD 43–44. Excavations within the remarkably complete walls have revealed the internal arrangement of the town, though all you will see now are fruitful fields (see Walk on page 114). The square, or forum, stood at the town centre with the basilica, forbear of the town hall, on one side and shops on the other three. The baths lay to the southeast and there were, of course, several temples and a great number of houses. Interestingly, a tiny building near the forum seems to have been an early Christian church. Beyond the walls, to the southeast, stands the impressive amphitheatre which held between 5,000 and 9,000 spectators and was used for sports and gladiatorial blood lettings. The little museum at Silchester Common has a small display, but most of the finds are in Reading Museum.

Silchester was an important Roman town and a communications centre from which roads radiated, quite literally, to all points of the compass. Yet today there is very little there, a place that has died but not quite vanished, lying amid a maze of lost little country lanes that twist and turn confusingly, as if mocking the Roman road engineers.

A CYCLE TOUR AROUND SILCHESTER

This 9-mile (14.4-km) tour starts at Bramley and takes the minor road northeast towards Fair Oak Green. Turn left where five roads meet and continue to Butlers Lands. Turn left here on to the Devil's Highway, the old Roman road from London to Silchester, eventually veering off to the left on the approach to Silchester. Walk across the site and imagine this as a thriving 3rd-century town. Follow the road round the wall to Silchester village and the Calleva Museum, which has a display of relics. Head southeast to Three Ashes and then turn south through Latchmere Green to Bramley Corner. Turn right back into

Roman walls follow the line of an earlier earthwork

A Walk Around Roman Calleva

An educational stroll exploring the old walls of Calleva Roman Town and its small museum, as well as the surrounding field and woodland paths. Generally level, but a few of the tracks can be muddy.

Time: 2 hours (longer if exploring the walls and museum).
Distance: 4 miles (6.4km).
Location: 6 miles (9.7km) north of Basingstoke.
Start: Park at Silchester church (by the old walls).
(OS grid ref: SU643623.)
OS Map: Explorer 159 (Reading, Wokingham & Pangbourne)
1:25,000.
See Key to Walks on page 121.

ROUTE DIRECTIONS

From the car park close to the perimeter wall of **Calleva** and the attractively positioned **Church of St Mary the Virgin**, turn left along Church Lane. Proceed to where the lane bears sharp left at the post box to visit the **Roman Amphitheatre**, signed through the kissing gate opposite.

Return back along the lane and take the waymarked bridleway right alongside Old Manor Farm. Go through a gate, continuing along a wide fenced trackway, which cuts across the centre of the Roman Town. At the perimeter walls proceed straight on, then turn right, then left through a gate along a fenced path. Proceed to the Roman Town car park and

bear left to the lane.

Cross over the lane and walk down an arrowed 'byway', and follow this often muddy old track to a lane. Bear right uphill, passing the Red Lion pub, then cross the waymarked stile on the left beside the Old School House. Descend through woodland, crossing duckboards, bear left at a T-junction of paths and cross a wooden footbridge across a stream. Your path follows the fringe of Benyon's Inclosure (yellow arrow), then at a stony track, turn right and follow it left at a fork of routes, downhill through woodland.

Soon bear left across a causeway by a lake and bear left where the track veers right. Shortly, pass beside a wooden barrier, then just beyond a house called 'Little Heath', and before the lane, bear sharp right on to a waymarked path through the edge of woodland. Climb a stile, then keep to the right-hand edge of pasture to a gate and stile in the far hedge and turn right along a lane. In 200 yards (182 metres), turn left signed 'Silchester'.

Bear left along Bramley Road and soon turn left on to a waymarked bridleway and pass the **Calleva Museum**. Continue along the pitted

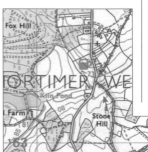

track, cross a stile beyond a row of cottages, ignore the arrowed stile left, and pass through a small gate on to the old walls of Calleva. Turn right through a further gate on to a tree-bordered path, eventually emerging on to the grassy path between the flint-layered wall and a wire fence. (It is possible to walk along the top of the bank.) Remain on this path back to the church and car park.

POINTS OF INTEREST

Calleva Roman Town
The important Roman encampment of Calleva Atrebatum lies at the northeast end of the Portway, the Roman road from Salisbury. The shape of the defences can still be traced on the ground and a section of the wall, nearly 2 miles (3.2 km) long, faces the medieval church. The walls once contained a prosperous market town and administrative centre with a population of around 4,000.

St Mary's Church, Silchester
Standing just inside the old walls, near the east gate, this attractive, largely unrestored church dates from the 12th century. It has an unusual layout with a long chancel and a short nave with aisles. Other notable features include 13th-century paintings and a fine organ of about 1770.

The pleasing old, white-washed Church of St Mary, Silchester

Roman Amphitheatre
Built in the 1st century AD, this well-excavated theatre could hold between 5,000 and 9,000 spectators who came to watch sport, gladiatorial contests, wild beast shows and public executions.

Roman Museum
Archaelogical finds from Victorian excavations of the site are on display here, along with a pictorial history of the town. Other finds can be seen at the museum in Reading.

Gardens and extensive parkland surround the mansion of Stratfield Saye

THE VICTOR OF WATERLOO
Arthur Wellesley, the 1st Duke of Wellington, must be one of the most famous of British soldiers, the man who finally crushed Napoleon at the Battle of Waterloo in 1815. Nicknamed the 'Iron Duke', Wellington was not a man to win great affection but he certainly had the respect of his troops. There is a marked contrast with the great naval hero of the time, Vice Admiral Lord Nelson, who earned not only the respect but also the love of his men. Nelson died at his victory, but Wellington survived for 37 years beyond his, and even served as Prime Minister. Nelson's Column is in London, Wellington's column, the Wellington Monument, stands at the eastern gates of his estate, a towering column topped by a statue of the duke in his Field Marshall's uniform.

STRATFIELD SAYE Map ref SU6861
In the year 1817 this pleasant mid 17th-century house was chosen by the Duke of Wellington, victor of Waterloo, as his gift from a grateful nation. At the time many felt that it was too modest a purchase for the man who had subdued and broken Napoleon, but the Iron Duke had intended to knock it down and build something grander. He even engaged architects, but for some reason he changed his mind.

Stratfield Saye is a long, low house, two storeys high with big Dutch gabled wings. It is built of brick, rendered and stuccoed, and is in some respects a rather quirky house. Not surprisingly it is full of Wellington relics: his library, with many books that had belonged to Napoleon, banners, flags, busts, paintings of the Peninsular War, his magnificent funeral carriage and a whole room given over to the memory of Copenhagen, the Duke's great war horse (whose grave is out in the grounds). An exhibition in the stable block portrays Wellington's life.

Wellington Country Park, to the east, covers 350 acres and is based on a lake with facilities for boating, windsurfing and fishing. There are nature trails in the woodlands, a deer park, a children's animal farm and a miniature railway.

THE VYNE Map ref SU6656
This magnificent Tudor house, built in 1515–27 for Henry VIII's Lord Chamberlain, Lord William Sandys, is pleasantly situated in the little valley of a tributary of the River Loddon. After the Civil War the impoverished Sandys family sold it to Chaloner Chute, who became

Speaker of the House of Commons in 1659. Chute added the classical portico to the north front – the first of its kind in England – and his great grandson, John, was responsible for further exterior alterations, including the canted bays at the ends of the wings.

The Vyne's best room must be the long gallery, complete with its original linenfold panelling, but with a wonderful rococo plaster ceiling. The chapel, described as 'the perfect example of a rich man's oratory of the 1520s', is particularly moving, with contemporary stained glass and encaustic tiles by Italian émigrés. John Chute engaged Thomas Carter the Younger to create a monument to his great grandfather, Chaloner, and this noble piece of 18th-century sculpture is a superb monument.

YATELEY COMMON COUNTRY PARK
Map ref SU8161

This 500-acre common near the northeastern county boundary is known for the wide variety of habitats to be found in spite of its proximity to the large military towns. The Hampshire/Berkshire boundary runs along the River Blackwater and at Wyndham Pool there is a nature trail and picnic site. Other habitats include gorse thickets, bogs and oak and birch woods. The country park is well known for bird watching since rare Dartford warblers have been known to breed here. You are more likely to see linnets, stonechats and goldfinches, and there is a resident population of birds of prey. Dragonflies and many different butterflies may be seen.

SPEAKER CHUTE
Chaloner Chute was a successful barrister when he purchased The Vyne during Oliver Cromwell's Protectorate. He was a large, genial man, as is apparent from his portrait by Van Dyck which hangs in the house. He was also noted for his spirited defence of his clients, his fair-mindedness and for his great wit. Recognised as a moderate, he was an obvious choice as Speaker of the House of Commons during the short-lived Protectorate of Oliver Cromwell's son, Richard. Clarendon, the great historian, commented that Chute 'would never have subjected himself to that place had he not entertained some hope of being able to serve the king', but he died in 1659, the year before the Restoration of Charles II.

The Vyne is a favourite National Trust property

The Northeast Heathlands

Leisure Information

Places of Interest

Shopping

The Performing Arts

Sports, Activities

and the Outdoors

Annual Events and Customs

✔ **Checklist**

Leisure Information

TOURIST INFORMATION CENTRES

Aldershot
Aldershot Military Museum, Queen's Avenue. Tel: 01252 320968.
Basingstoke
The Willis Museum, Old Town Hall. Tel: 01256 817618.
Fleet
The Hartlington Centre, Fleet Road. Tel: 01252 811151.

OTHER INFORMATION

Countryside Commission
John Dower House, Crescent Place, Cheltenham, Gloucester. Tel: 01242 521381.
English Heritage
Eastgate Court, 195–205 High Street, Guildford, Surrey. Tel: 01483 252000.
www.english-heritage.org.uk
Hampshire and Isle of Wight Wildlife Trust
8 Romsey Road, Eastleigh. Tel: 02380 613636.
Environment Agency
Southern Region, Guildbourne House, Chatsworth Road, Worthing, Sussex. Tel: 01903 832000.
National Trust
Southern Region, Polesden Lacey, Dorking, Surrey.
Tel: 01372 453401.
www.nationaltrust.org.uk
RSPB
South East Regional Office, 2nd Floor, 42 Frederic Place, Brighton, West Sussex. Tel: 01273 763600.

ORDNANCE SURVEY MAPS

Landranger 1:50,000. Sheet numbers: 174, 175, 185, 186.

Places of Interest

Admission is charged unless otherwise stated.
Airborne Forces Museum
Browning Barracks, Queens Avenue, Aldershot. Tel: 01252 349619. Open all year, daily.
Aldershot Military Museum
Evelyn Woods Road, Queen's Avenue, Aldershot. Tel: 01252 314598. Open all year, daily ex 2 weeks Christmas & New Year.
Basing House
Redbridge Lane, Old Basing. Tel: 01256 467294. Open Apr–Sep, most days.
Calleva Museum
Bramley Road, Silchester. Tel: 01962 846735. Open all year, daily. Free.
Milestones
Leisure Park, Churchill Way West, Basingstoke. Tel: 01256 477766. Open all year, Tue–Sun & Bank Hol Mon.
Stratfield Saye House
Off A33. Tel: 01256 882882. Open Jun–Sep, most days.
The Vyne
Sherborne St John. Tel: 01256 881337. Open late Mar–Sep, most days.
Wellington Country Park and National Dairy Museum
Riseley, off B3349. Tel: 0118 932 6444. Open Mar–Oct, daily, weekends Nov–Feb.
Willis Museum
Market Place, Old Town Hall, Basingstoke. Tel: 01256 465902. Open all year, most days. Free.

SPECIAL INTEREST FOR CHILDREN

The following may be of interest to visitors with children.
Wellington Country Park and National Dairy Museum
Riseley, off B3349. Tel: 0118 932 6444. Open Mar–Oct, daily, weekends Nov–Feb.

Shopping

Aldershot
Open-air market, town centre, Thu. Wellington Shopping Centre.
Basingstoke
Open-air market in old market square, Wed and Sat. Large pedestrianised shopping area.

Farnborough
Open-air market, town centre.
Kingsmead Shopping Centre,
The Princes Mead.
Fleet
Open-air market, town centre,
Sat. The Hart Shopping Centre.

LOCAL SPECIALITIES
Craft Centre
The Viables, The Harrow Way,
Basingstoke. Tel: 01256 473634.
Open all year, Tue–Sat.

The Performing Arts

Haymarket Theatre
Wote Street, Basingstoke. Tel:
01256 465566.
The Anvil
Churchill Way, Basingstoke. Tel:
01256 844244.
Prince Regent Theatre
75 Guildford Road East,
Farnborough. Tel: 01252
510859.
West End Centre
Queen's Road, Aldershot. Tel:
01252 330040

Sports, Activities and the Outdoors

ANGLING
Coarse
There is fishing along the
Basingstoke Canal; contact the
Visitor Centre, Mychett Place
Road, Mytchett, Surrey. Tel:
01252 370073.

CANAL TRIPS
Odiham
Summer trips on the Basingstoke
Canal from Colt Hill Bridge. Tel:
01962 713564 for bookings.

COUNTRY PARKS, FORESTS AND NATURE RESERVES
Ancells Farm, west of Aldershot.
Fleet Pond Nature Reserve, near
Fleet.
Yateley Common Country Park.
Tel: 01252 874346.

CRICKET
Basingstoke
County Cricket is played at Mays
Bounty ground, off Winchester
Road.

GOLF COURSES
Aldershot
Army Golf Club, Laffans Road.
Tel: 01252 337272.
Basingstoke
Basingstoke Golf Club,
Kempshott Park. Tel: 01256
465990.
Dummer
Dummer Golf Club. Tel: 01256
397888.
Farnborough
Southwood Golf Course, Ively
Road. Tel: 01252 548700.
Fleet
North Hants Golf Club, The
Clubhouse, Minley Road. Tel:
01252 616443.
Hartley Witney
Hartley Witney Golf Club,

London Road. Tel: 01252
844211.
Kingsclere
Sandford Springs, on A339
Kingsclere bypass. Tel: 01635
296800.
Rotherwick
Tylney Park Golf Club.
Tel: 01256 762079.
Sherborne St John
Weybrook Park, Rooksdown
Lane, Aldermaston Road.
Tel: 01256 320347.
Tadley
Bishopswood Golf Club,
Bishopswood Lane, Tadley.
Tel: 0118 981 2200.

GOLF DRIVING RANGE
Basingstoke
Basingstoke Golf Centre.
Tel: 01256 350054.

Annual Events and Customs

Farnborough
Farnborough Air Show, held
every two years.
Stratfield Saye
Wellington Country Park
Country Fair, mid-July.
Shetland Pony Show, Wellington
Country Park, September.

A Chieftain tank outside the Aldershot Military Museum

Atlas and Map Symbols

THE NATIONAL GRID SYSTEM

The National Grid system covers Great Britain with an imaginary network of 100 kilometre grid squares. Each square is given a unique alphabetic reference as shown in the diagram. These squares are sub-divided into one hundred 10 kilometre squares, each numbered from 0 to 9 in an easterly (left to right) direction and northerly (upwards) direction from the bottom left corner. Each 10 km square is similarly sub-divided into one hundred 1 km squares.

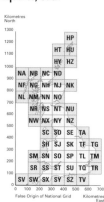

KEY TO ATLAS

⛪	Abbey, cathedral or priory	– – – –	National trail
🐟	Aquarium	NT	National Trust property
♜	Castle	NTS	National Trust for Scotland property
⌒	Cave	🦌	Nature reserve
♛	Country park	★	Other place of interest
🏏	County cricket ground	P+R	Park and Ride location
🐄	Farm or animal centre	⛏	Picnic site
⋯⋯	Forest drive	🚂	Steam centre
❀	Garden	🎿	Ski slope natural
⛳	Golf course	🎿	Ski slope artifical
🏰	Historic house	🅘	Tourist Information Centre
🐎	Horse racing	☼	Viewpoint
🏁	Motor racing	🅥	Visitor or heritage centre
🏛	Museum	🐟	Zoological or wildlife collection
☎	AA telephone		Forest Park
✈	Airport		Heritage coast
Ⓗ	Heliport		National Park (England & Wales)
🗼	Windmill		National Scenic Area (Scotland)

KEY TO TOURS

🚗	Tour start point	Buckland Abbey	Highlighted point of interest
➡	Direction of tour		
▪▪▶▮▶	Optional detour	⟋⟍	Featured tour

KEY TO ATLAS

MOTORWAY

M4	Motorway with number	A1123	Other A road single/dual carriageway
Fleet	Motorway service area	⊨=====⊨	Road tunnel
1	Motorway junction with and without number	Toll	Toll
3	Restricted motorway junctions		Road under construction
⊫⊐⊏⊒	Motorway and junction under construction	⊹	Roundabout

PRIMARY ROUTE

A3	Primary route single/dual carriageway	B2070	B road single/dual carriageway
Grantham North	Primary route service area	⊹	B road interchange junction
BATH	Primary route destinations	⊹	B road roundabout with adjoining unclassified road
⊹	Roundabout		Steep gradient
▼ 5 ▲	Distance in miles between symbols		Unclassified road single/dual carriageway
══════	Narrow Primary route with passing places	—○—✕—	Railway station and level crossing

A ROAD

B ROAD

KEY TO WALKS

Scale 1:25,000, 2½ inches to 1 mile, 4cm to 1 km

	Start of walk		Line of walk
→	Direction of walk	‖▸‖▸▸‖▸	Optional detour
		Buckland Abbey	Highlighted point of interest

ROADS AND PATHS

M1 or A6(M)	M1 or A6(M)	Motorway
A 31(T) or A35	A 31(T) or A35	Trunk or main road
B 3074	B 3074	Secondary road
A 35	A 35	Dual carriageway
		Road generally more than 4m wide
		Road generally less than 4m wide
		Other road, drive or track
		Path

Unfenced roads and tracks are shown by pecked lines

RAILWAYS

Multiple track	Standard gauge		Embankment
Single track			Tunnel
Narrow gauge			Road over; road under
Siding			Level crossing
Cutting			Station

PUBLIC RIGHTS OF WAY

Public rights of way may not be evident on the ground

Public paths	footpath bridleway	Byway open to all traffic
Permissive path		Road used as a public path
Permissive bridleway		Named path
	Pennine Way	National trail or recreational path

The representation on this map of any other road, track or path is no evidence of the existence of a right of way

RELIEF

50 ·	Heights determined by	Ground survey
285 ·		Air survey

Contours are at 5 and 10 metres vertical interval

SYMBOLS

	Place of worship	with tower	○ W, Spr Well, Spring
		with spire, minaret or dome	Gravel pit
		without such additions	
			Other pit or quarry
	Building		
	Important building		Sand pit
· T; A; R	Telephone: public; AA; RAC		Refuse or slag heap
--□---- pylon pole	Electricity transmission line		County Boundary (England & Wales)
△ △	Triangulation pillar		
	Bus or coach station		Water
Ⱶ Ⱶ	Lighthouse; beacon		Sand; sand & shingle
⊹	Site of antiquity		National Park boundary
NT	National Trust always open		
FC	Forestry Commission		Mud

DANGER AREA

Firing and test ranges in the area
Danger!
Observe warning notices

VEGETATION

Limits of vegetation are defined by positioning of the symbols but may be delineated also by pecks or dots

	Coniferous trees		Non-coniferous trees
	Orchard		Heath
	Coppice		Marsh, reeds, saltings.

TOURIST AND LEISURE INFORMATION

⋏	Camp site	PC	Public convenience
ℹ	Information centre	🅿	Parking
ℹ	Information centre (seasonal)	☆	Viewpoint
	Caravan site	⊕	Mountain rescue post
✕	Picnic site		

Index

Acknowledgements

The author would like to thank the various tourist offices within Hampshire and the Isle of Wight for their assistance.
Second edition verified by David Hancock.

The Automobile Association wishes to thank the following photographers and libraries for their assistance in the preparation of this book.

NATURE PHOTOGRAPHERS LTD 6e (P R Sterry), 7d (R O Bush), 7h (E A Janes)
THE MANSELL COLLECTION LTD 6c, 6g, 7f

All remaining pictures are held in the Association's own library (AA PHOTO LIBRARY) with contributions from the following photographers:

M ADLEMAN 18; **D CROUCHER** 3f, 3g, 3h, 3i, 3j, 6a, 7e, 14, 77a, 77b, 78, 79, 80, 81, 82, 83, 84, 85, 86, 87, 88, 90, 92a, 93, 94, 95, 96, 97, 98, 99, 100, 102, 104, 105a, 105b, 107, 108a, 108b, 110, 113, 115, 116, 117, 119; **P EDEN** 72; **D FORSS** 3a, 3b, 3c, 3d, 3e, 6b, 6f, 7a, 7b, 8/9, 8a, 8b, 9a, 9b, 9c, 9d, 9e, 10/11, 10a, 10b, 11a, 11c, 12a, 12b, 16, 17, 20, 22, 23, 25, 26, 27, 28, 30, 31, 33, 35, 37a, 37b, 38, 39, 40, 41, 42, 43, 44, 45, 48, 49, 50, 54a, 54b, 56, 59, 61, 62, 63, 64, 65, 67a, 67b, 68, 69, 70, 71; **S & O MATHEWS** 55; **K PATERSON** 7c; **W VOYSEY** 6d, 7g, 13, 19, 47, 57, 60, 92b, 109, 111, 112